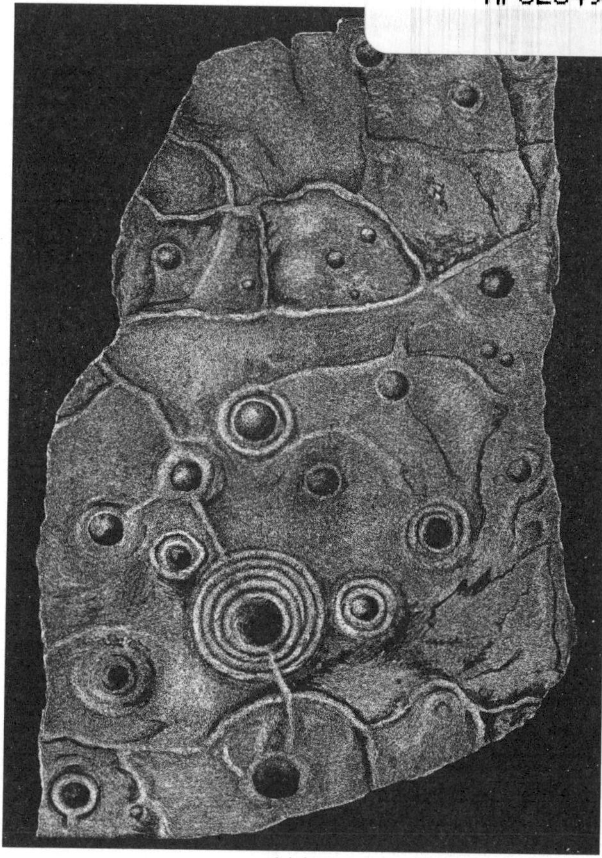

Slab from Sneem in the County of Kerry, Ireland

First published 2007
This edition © Wooden Books Ltd 2022

Published by Wooden Books Ltd.
Glastonbury, Somerset
www.woodenbooks.com·

British Library Cataloguing in Publication Data
Mansell, C.
Ancient British Rock Art

A CIP catalogue record for this book
may be obtained from the British Library

ISBN-10: 1-904263-56-9
ISBN-13: 978-1-904263-56-2

Designed and typeset in Glastonbury, UK.

Printed in China on FSC® certified papers by
RR Donnelley Asia Printing Solutions Ltd.

ANCIENT BRITISH
ROCK ART

A GUIDE TO INDIGENOUS STONE CARVINGS

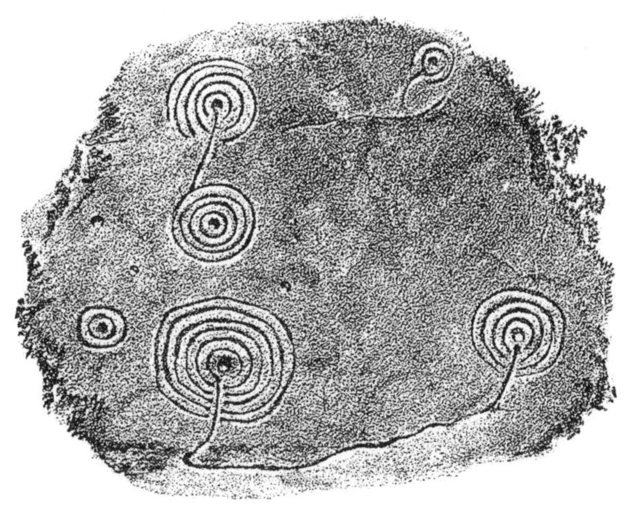

Chris Mansell

*I would like to dedicate this book to Chujé Akong Rinpoché
and would especially like to thank my dear friends Sandra Berwald and John Martineau
for their help and support in the production of this small directory of ancient art.*

*Further reading: "British Prehistoric Rock Art" by Stan Beckensall (1999), "The Carved Rocks
on Rombald's Moor" by the Ilkley Archaeology Group (1986), "Images of Prehistory" by Peter
Fowler & Mick Sharp (1990), "Kilmartin" by the Royal Commission on the Ancient Historical
Monuments of Scotland (1999), "The Stars and the Stones" Martin Brennan (1983)*

*Illustrations are from James Fergusson's "Rude Stone Monuments" (1872), Llewellynn Jewitt's
"Grave Mounds and their Contents" (1870), Sir J. Y. Simpson's "Archaic Sculpturings"
(1867), George Tate's "Ancient British Sculptured Rocks …" (1865), Algernon, Duke of
Northumberland's "Incised Markings in Stone" (1869), E. T. Cowling's "Rombald's Way"
(1946), and Martin Brennan's "The Stars and The Stones" (1984). The illustration on this page,
the previous page and page 3 are all of Loughcrew, Eire. Occasional pictures are by the author.*

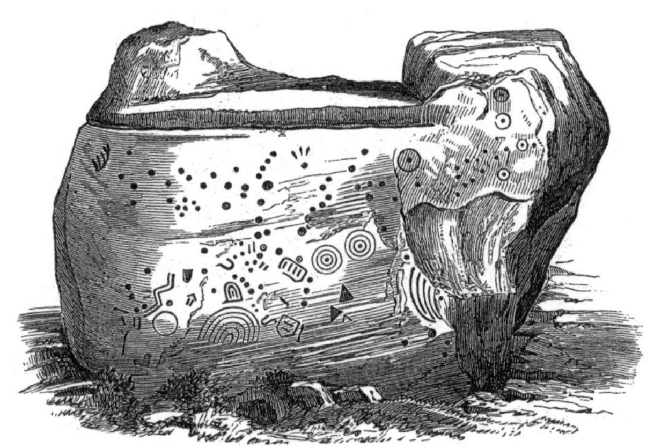

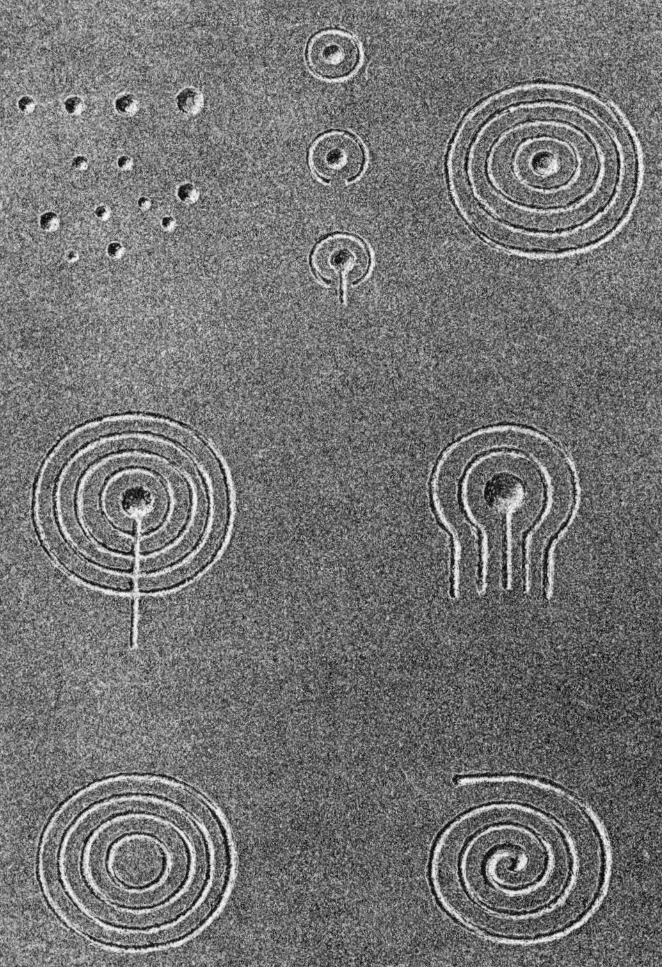

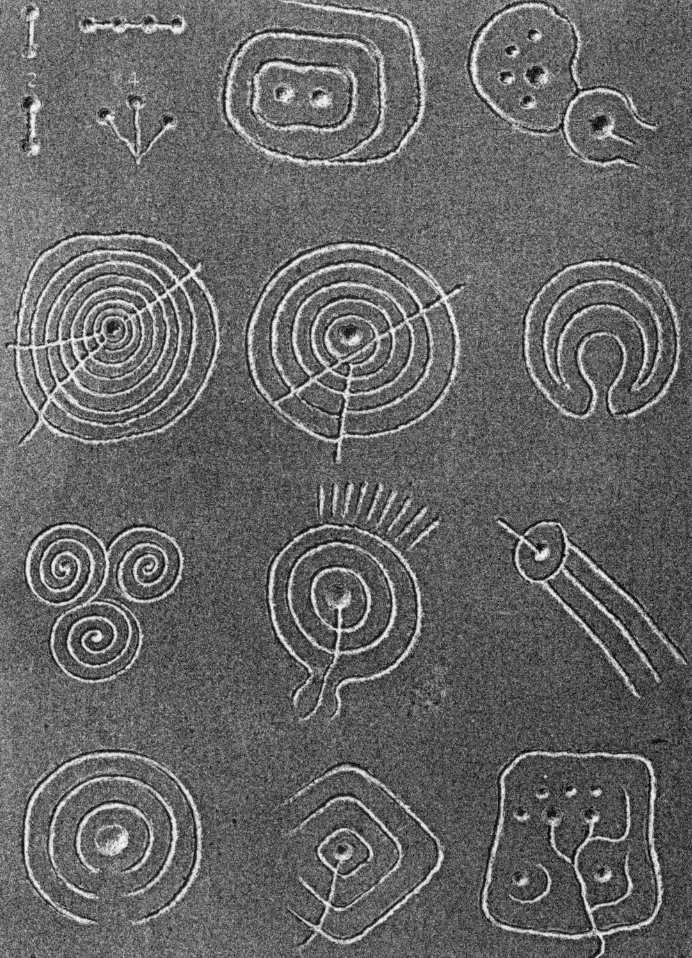

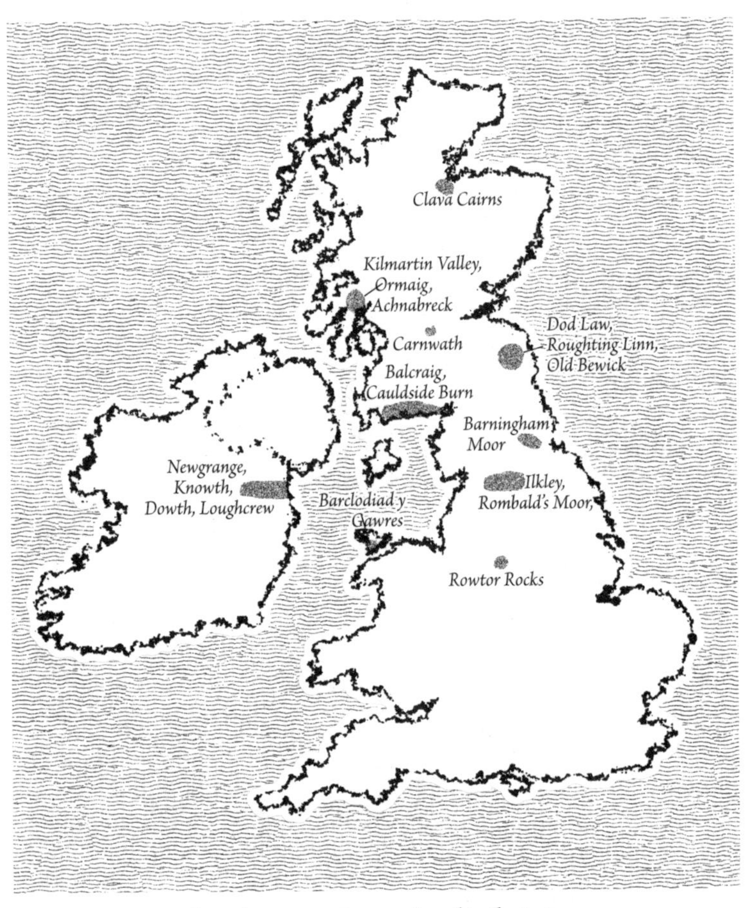

Some important sites mentioned in the text.

INTRODUCTION

SITTING ON A HILLSIDE at one particularly extensive site near Kilmartin, early on a warm summer's morning, waiting for the sun to rise above the pine forest and illuminate the wonderful range of carvings, I realised that there may never be any explanation for these ancient designs. I often feel that my own involvement with this subject is as much of a mystery as the images themselves. However, perhaps we are often so preoccupied with the process of rationalisation that we lose sight of our original attraction and involvement, which was, for me, largely aesthetic. On this occasion the simple fact of being in this remote and beautiful place, with these mysterious images, was explanation enough.

The Kilmartin Valley, in Argyllshire, is only one of many sites in Great Britain and Ireland which exhibit ancient rock carvings. Having visited this area some years earlier without time to explore some of the more remote sites I had always intended to return. There is, simply, a treasure chest of prehistoric features with decorated burial chambers, standing stones, stone alignments and circles and a wealth of rock carvings. It is almost like a gazetteer of the finest evidence of our ancient culture.

In Northumberland, Durham, Yorkshire, Derbyshire, Galloway in Scotland and in County Meath in Ireland there are also extensive examples of carvings displaying many different styles. It seems somewhat surprising that, while so much is made of the cave paintings at Altamira in Spain and at Lascaux in France, in our own environment exist some of the most mysterious, enigmatic and beautiful designs which, until fairly recent times, have gone largely unnoticed.

I can't remember exactly how I came to be aware of ancient rock carvings. I was born and lived in Durham for many years, totally unaware that within an hour's drive were excellent examples of prehistoric art, at Dod Law, Old Bewick and Roughting Linn in Northumberland, and at Barningham Moor in County Durham, I can only say that my joy at their discovery and my subsequent involvement has led me to an area of research which gives me continuous pleasure.

As an artist myself, my interest in rock art is largely visual, I do not claim to be an archaeological historian, but, as this seems to be a visual language, I think we can look at them as we would any other work of art.

I have been significantly inspired and fascinated by the research of people such as Stan Beckensall, Michael J. O'Kelly and Martin Brennan, and by organisations like the Ilkley Archaeology Group, the Royal Commission for Historic Monuments in Scotland, the Kilmartin House Museum and the Newgrange Museum in Ireland. If it was not for the excellent work and contribution of people such as these the subject would hardly be in evidence.

This book mainly covers examples of carvings from Great Britain and Ireland, but it is worth mentioning that rock art exists all over the world.

For me these drawings have a particular mystery and visual beauty which is impossible to assess, evidence of a bygone intelligence and culture, and it gives me great pleasure to share with those who look at this book some of that mystery and some of the time I have spent with this fascinating subject.

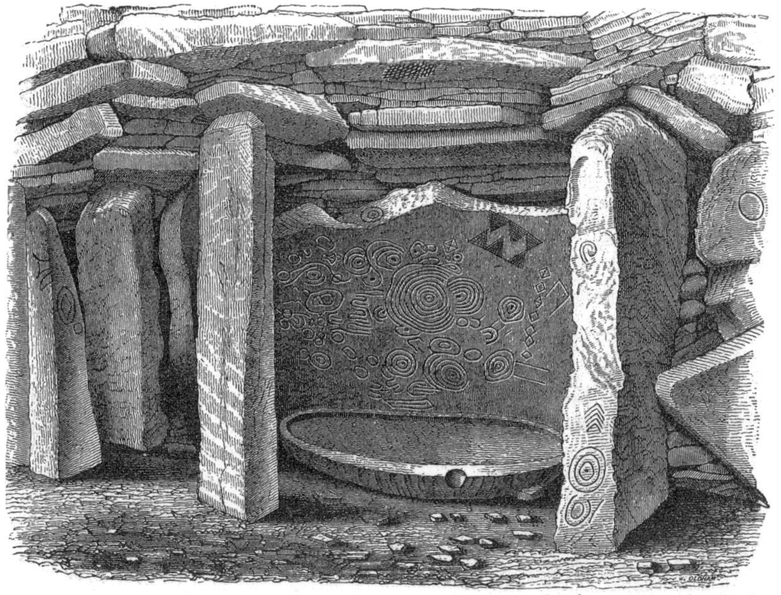

Loughcrew, Co. Meath, Ireland

DISTRIBUTION OF ROCK ART
an overview of primary sites and styles

THE FORMAL ELEMENTS of rock carvings exhibit many different styles. The most important sites covered in the text are shown in the map opposite page 1.

Locations often have similar types of carvings but also display unique drawings. Likewise, there is no hard and fast rule for the surfaces employed, but examples from Northern England and Scotland generally seem to occur on natural horizontal outcrops, while in Ireland and Anglesey the carvings appear on the walls of passage graves, or on individual vertical stones.

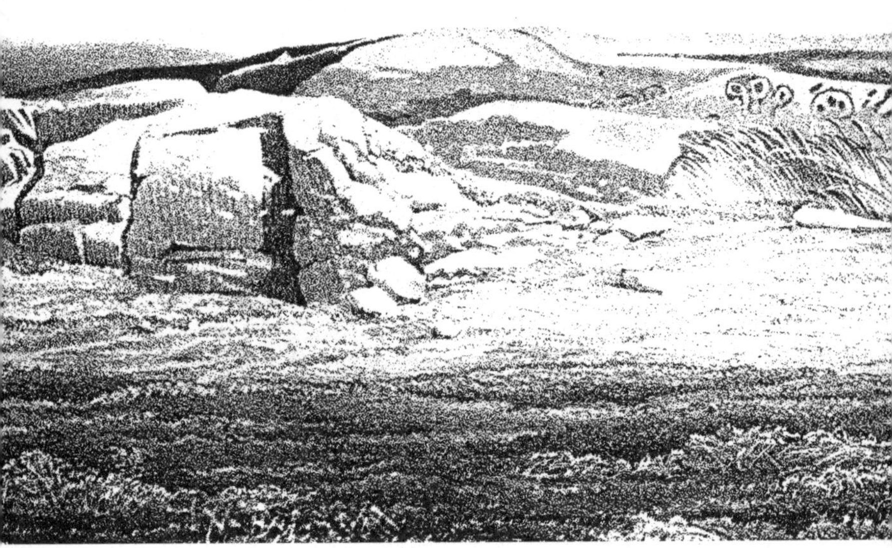

Many of the carvings found in passage graves are quite ornate, involving spirals and complex designs, while those on outdoor horizontal surfaces tend to involve cups and rings and more basic patterns.

Individual elements such as cups and sets of rings are usually fairly small, ranging from one to eight inches in diameter. However, multiple arrangements of carvings can cover many square yards as can be seen at Achnabreck in the Kilmartin Valley.

The drawings are thought to have been created by the process of "pecking", gradually chipping away the surface with a stone chisel from a basic scratch to a depth of about one inch.

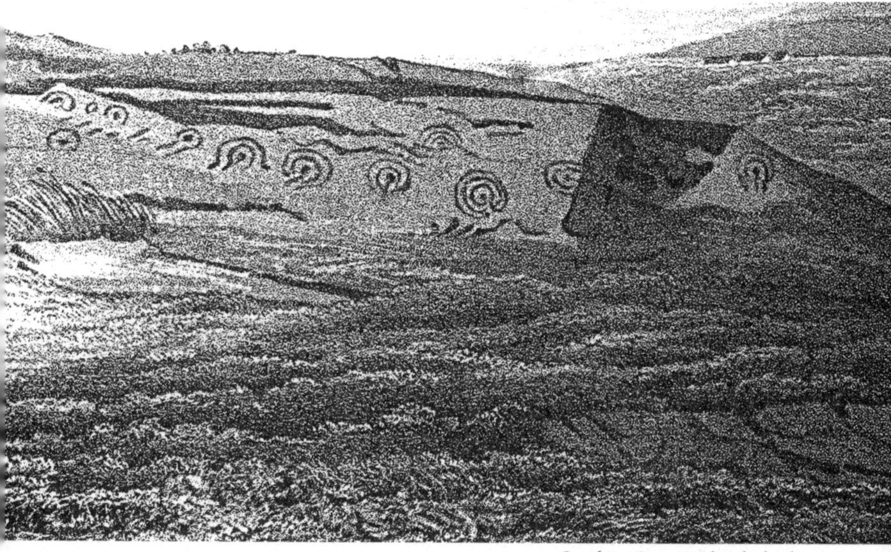

Roughting Linn, Northumberland

ROUGHTING LINN
Northumberland

The carvings shown here are from Roughting Linn, one of the largest known decorated outcrops, which exhibits a range of complex designs developed largely around the 'cup and ring' format. The illustration of the site on the previous page, produced for the Duke of Northumberland in 1869, shows the site as a bleak and remote outcrop in the middle of extensive moorland, a majestic feature in an empty landscape.

Today the site is bypassed by a road. Trees and bushes have grown up and it has been surrounded by a fence. It might seem that much of its original aesthetic relationship with the landscape has been lost, but, judging by the quantity of small offerings on view at every visit, this place is still special to many.

The sheer scale of Roughting Linn is testament to the fact that whoever produced these drawings was making a deliberate and significant statement.

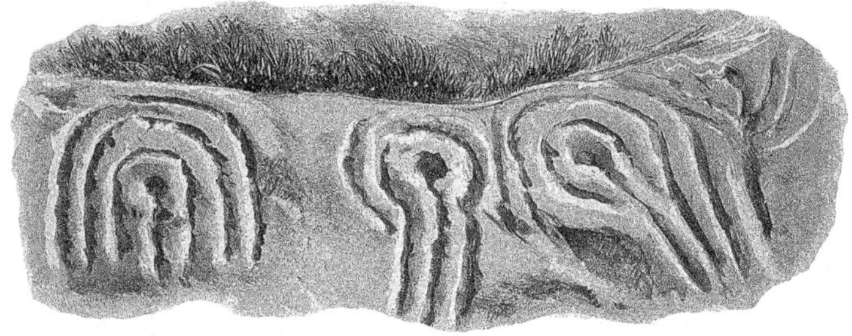

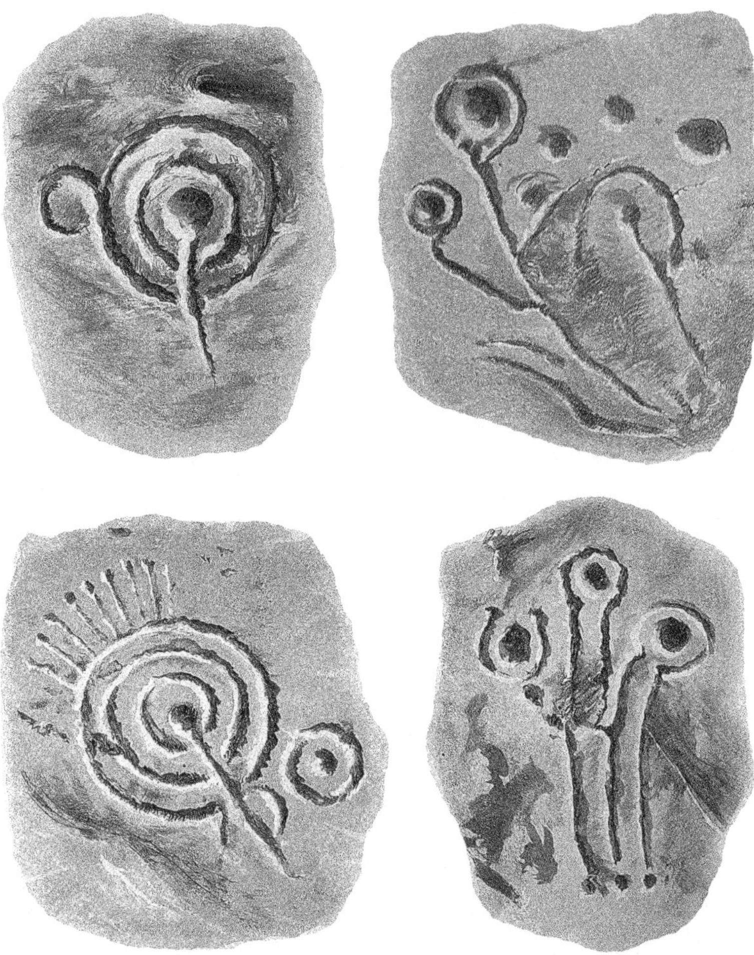

Cups and Rings

the basic motifs

"Cups and rings" is a generic term for a whole range of Neo-lithic and Bronze Age rock carvings dated to 2000-3000 BC.

In truth the simple phrase belies a whole range of styles and designs which have interested and intrigued researchers and enthusiasts since the last century. There are many different combinations of design elements to be found, and the existence of anomalies, such as the "ladder" forms found on Rombald's Moor, confounds the notion of an over-arching explanation.

Different sites throughout the British Isles also often exhibit specific innovations and motifs which may possibly be explained by influences from differing cultures, but the cup-and-ring format seems to be a common thread.

Many of the carvings are linked to contemporary cairns and burial mounds, but others can be found isolated on remote outcrops on empty moorland.

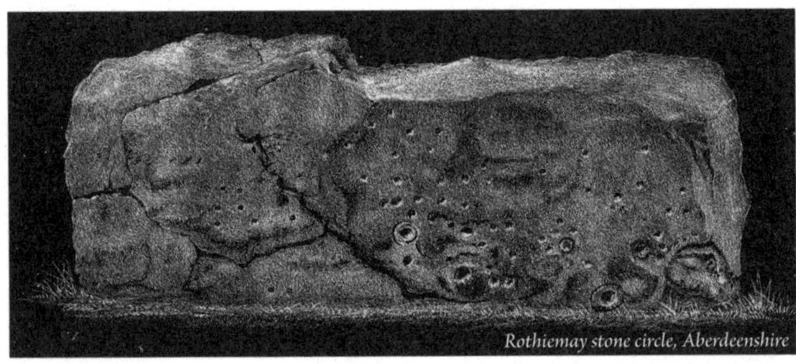

Rothiemay stone circle, Aberdeenshire

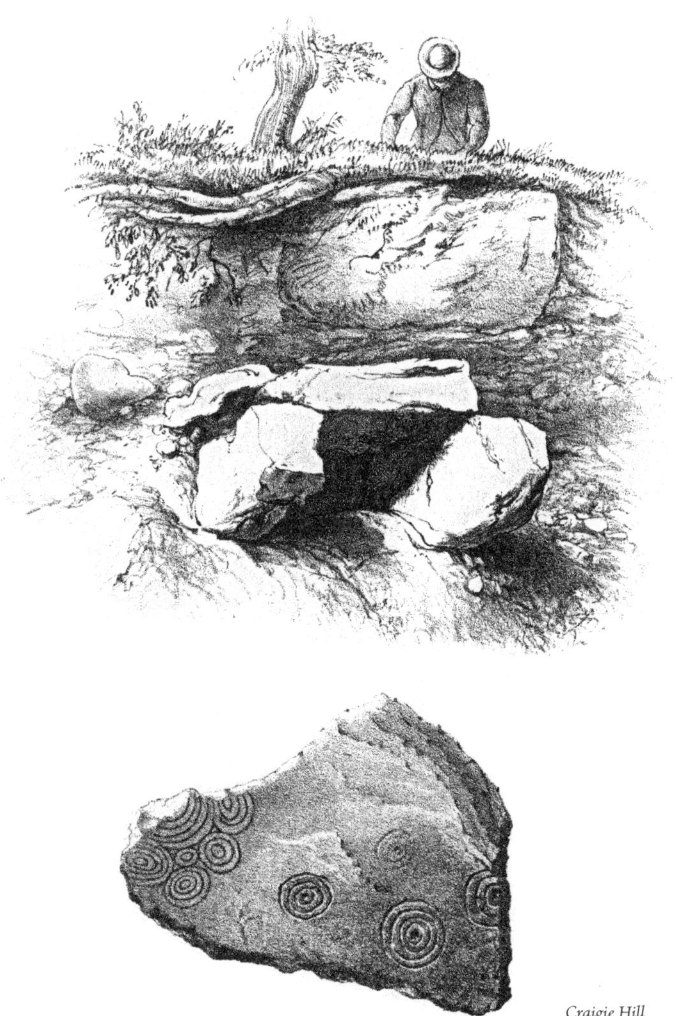

Craigie Hill

EARLY AND MODERN RESEARCH
from the 1860s until the present

It seems strange that the subject of ancient British rock art is so roundly ignored by the contemporary art world. We have to go back over 100 years, to the mid 19th century, before we find the last flurry of interest. In the 1860s a rash of publications appeared with detailed lithographs and drawings of these fascinating forms; there were books by G. Tate, Sir J. Y. Simpson and, at the request of the Duke of Northumberland, a large format series of plates based on surveys by J Collingwood Bruce. Popular interest spiked again in the 1880's before going underground in the 20th century.

In recent years the hard work and perseverance of Stan Beckensall has generated and maintained an interest in the subject and his considerable work in recording and archiving many carvings will long benefit others.

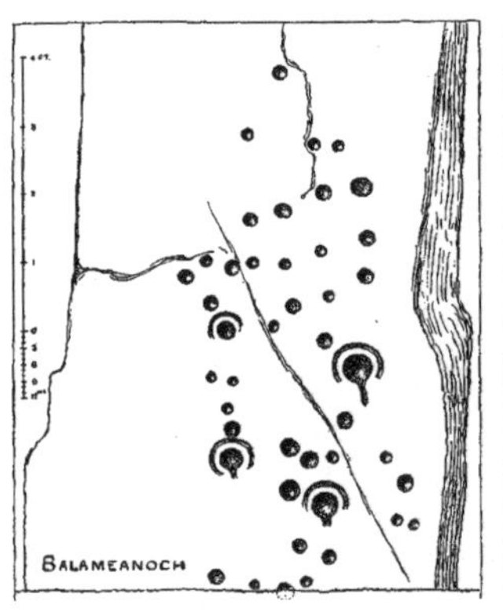

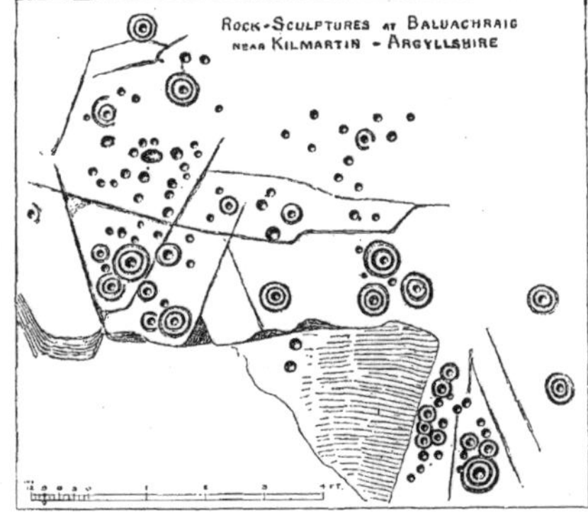

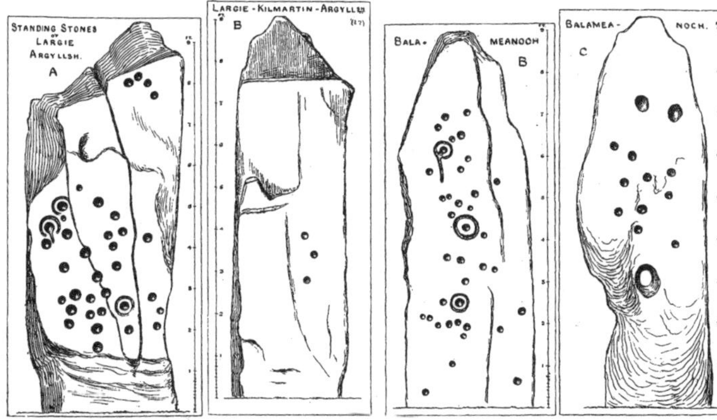

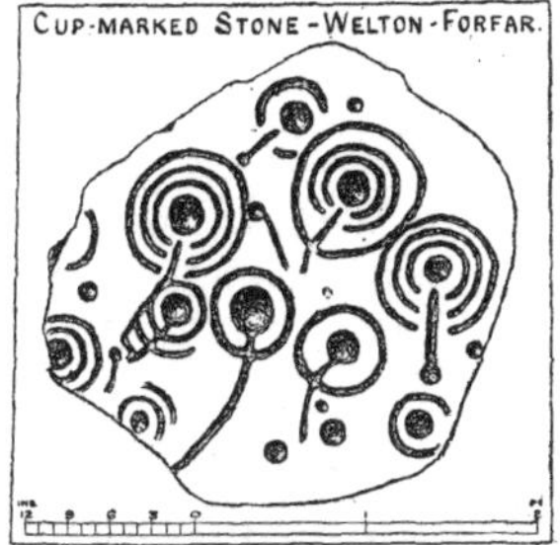

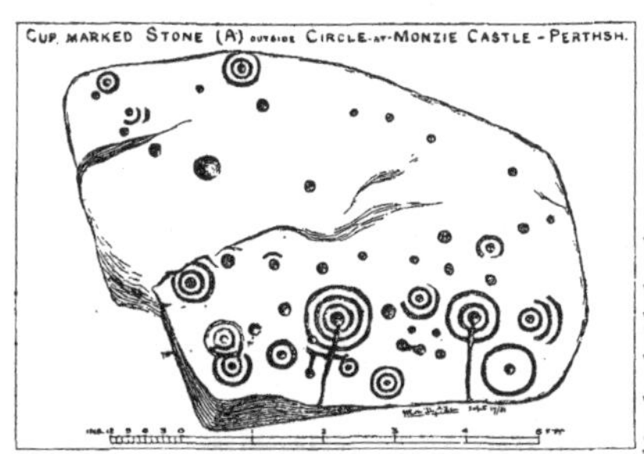

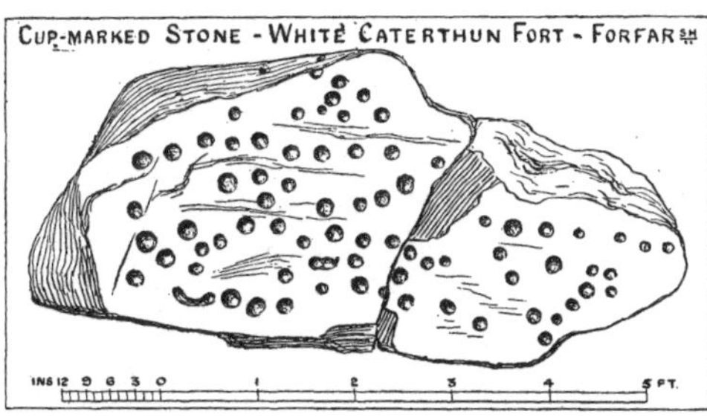

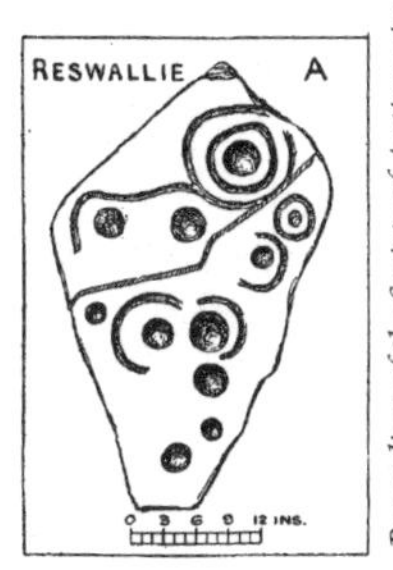

Proceedings of the Society of Antiquaries of Scotland, Edinburgh 1882

CUP MARKINGS
Clava Cairns, Invernesshire

The Clava Cairns, or Bulnaraun of Clava, consist of three cairns, two of which have passageways aligned to the southwestern midwinter sunset position. They may be found down a minor road off the B9006 from Inverness.

Cup marks are clearly visible on some of the stones, and their deliberate inclusion and arrangement within the overall design and structure of the site is strong evidence for their possessing some kind of significance and meaning.

The Clava Cairns group is one of the best examples of a Bronze Age burial complex in Scotland, each of the three cairns here being surrounded by a stone circle. The cup marks are to be found on the outer facing stones of the cairns, but it has been suggested that the carvings may be even older than the structure, the stones having been reused because of their special status.

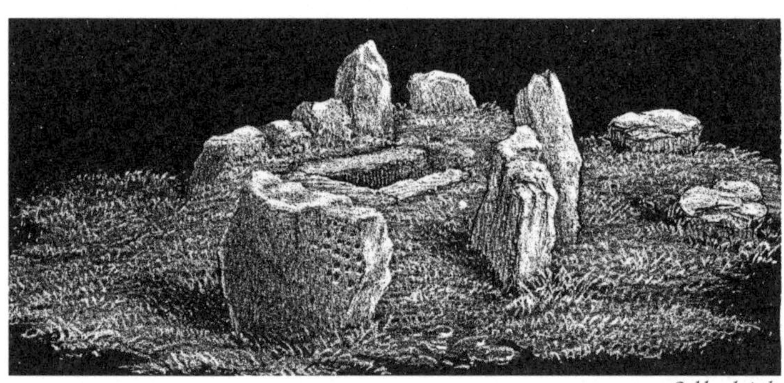

Oakland circle

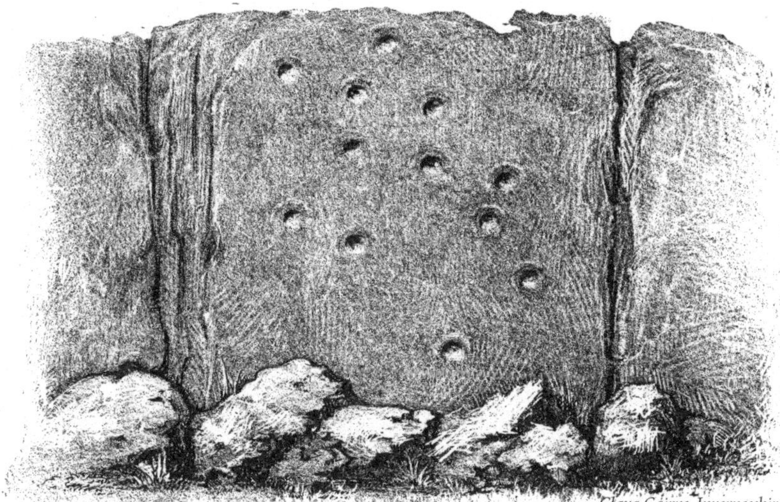

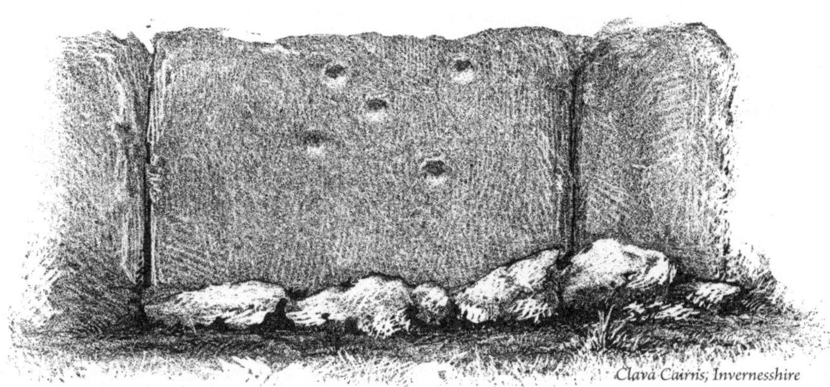

Clava Cairns, Invernesshire

Clava Cairns, Invernesshire

JOINED CUPS
Rosshire fragments

The joining together of discrete visual elements with varying types of pathway is a development seen at many locations (e.g., Ormaig and Old Bewick) and it is clear that there is some intention here in relating one element to another.

Cups and rings are also commonly found on horizontal outcrops, which has prompted suggestions that these joined motifs were used for water or blood in ritual processes in some way. However, at Ballochmyle in Ayrshire the carvings are found on a cliff face, so this would seem to contradict that theory. In looking at these designs it is additionally possible that some symbolic connection is being made between the joined elements. The seemingly random connections only add to the fascination of these drawings.

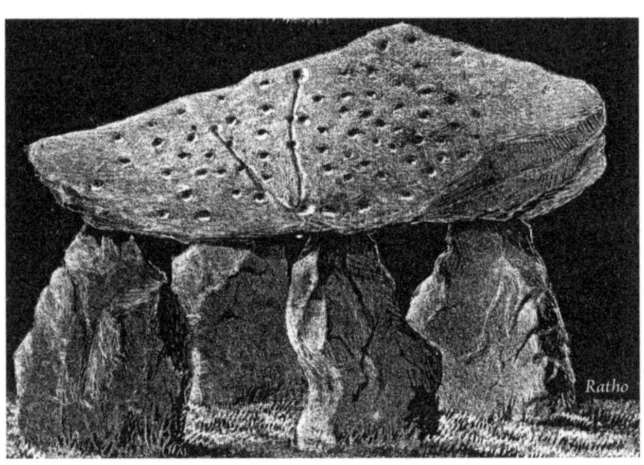

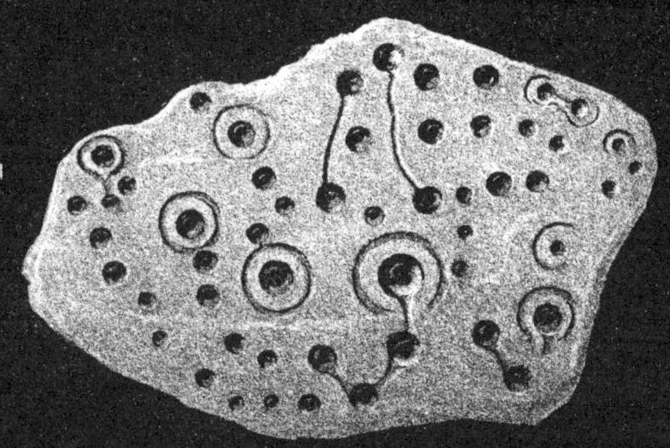

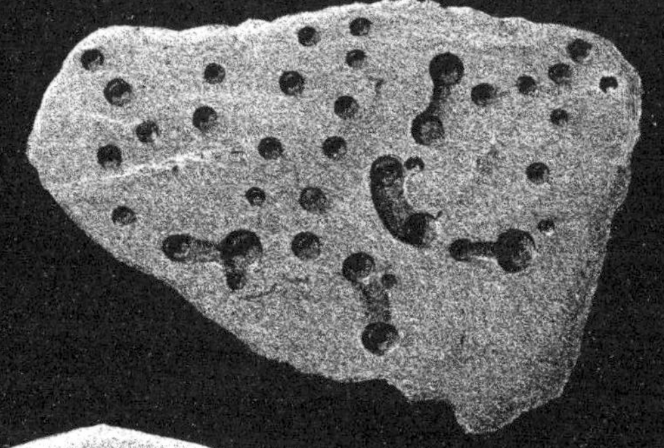

cups and rings from Rosshire

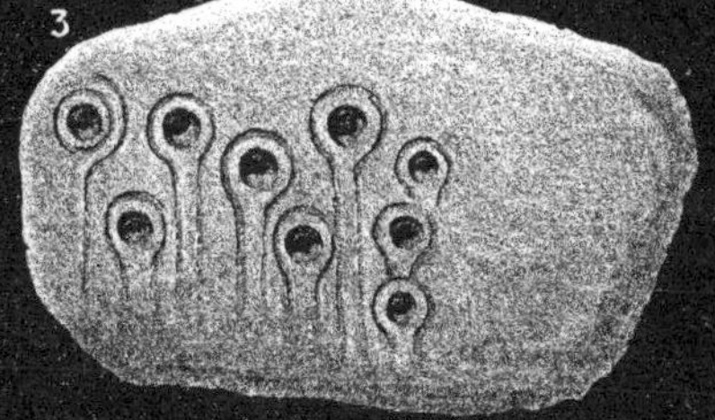

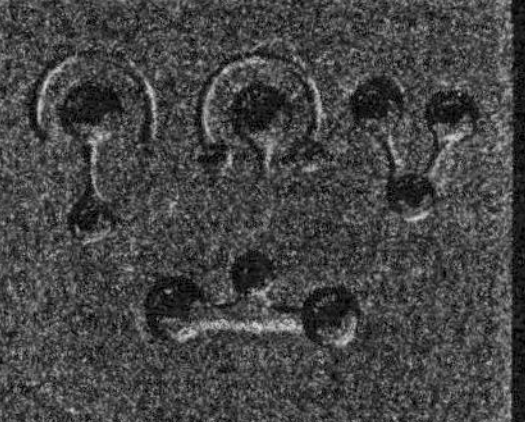

RINGED CUPS

Ballymenach Stones, Kilmartin Valley, Argyllshire

This site consists of an alignment of quite large standing stones, averaging about twelve feet, one being extensively decorated with cup and ring markings. There is a kerb cairn and a henge nearby. A modern drawing (with more detail than the 19th century lithograph opposite) is shown below.

It is impossible to tell whether these remaining stones were part of a larger arrangement, but they are somewhat reminiscent of the stone avenue at Avebury. The decorated stone is immediately significant in the sense that the carvings are not made on a horizontal surface as are the majority of examples in this area. It has therefore been suggested that the carvings may predate the stone's erection here, posing the question of its positional importance in relationship to its neighbours. The alignment is north-south.

The concept of the carvings being applied to a vertical stone would be evidence for the merging of two different processes, signs of which also occur nearby at Nether Largie.

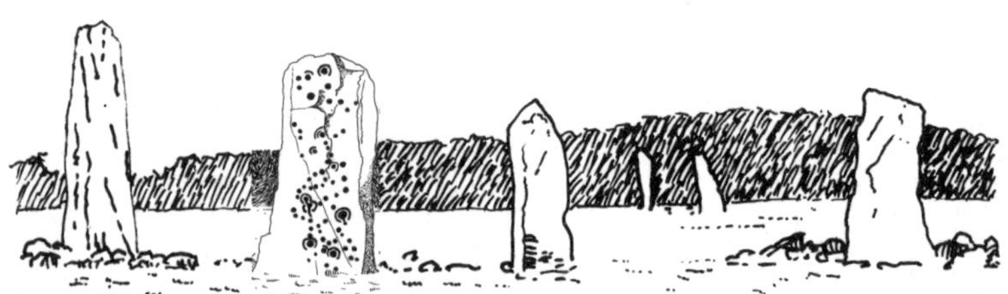

Ballymenach Stones, Kilmartin Valley, Argylleshire

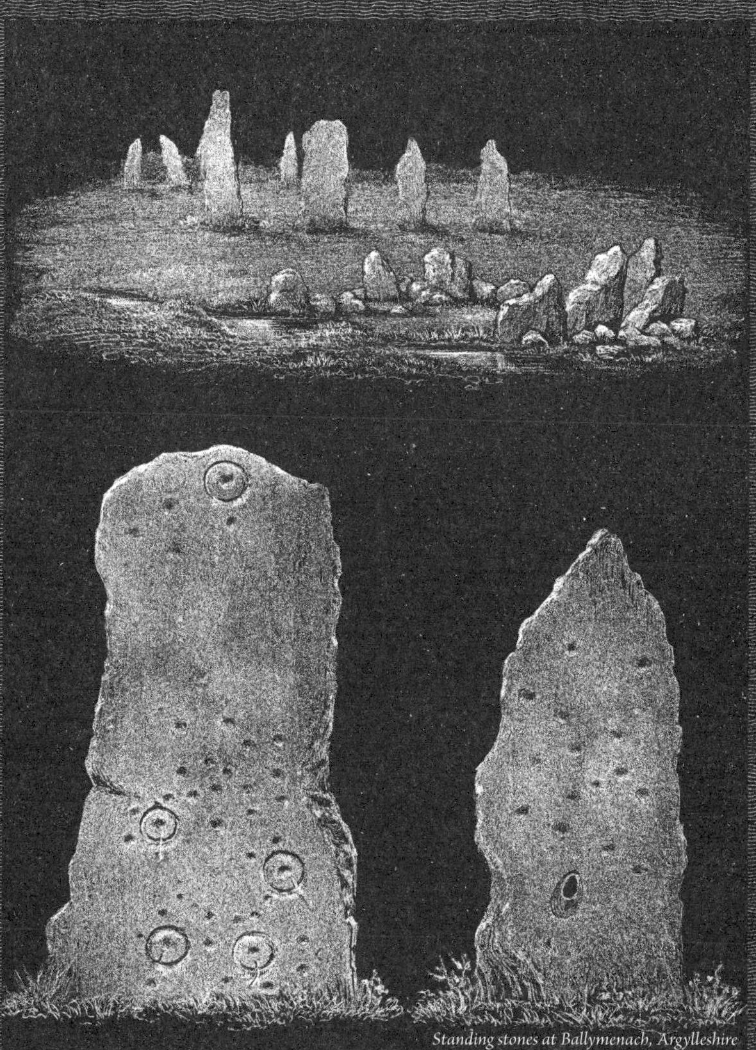

Standing stones at Ballymenach, Argylleshire

ENCLOSED CUPS & RECTANGLES

Dod Law, Northumberland & Rowtor Rocks, Derbyshire

The area surrounding Dod Law shows a great variety of carvings, once again on flat outcrops on the highest ground. The rectangular detail on the stone opposite does not include rings as a formal element and is an interesting diversion. There is reasonable evidence here to suggest the more diagrammatic or representational purpose of these designs. The motif could possibly relate to the plans of an enclosure or hillfort.

The pattern below, from Rowtor Rocks, interestingly includes cups and rings along with the visually more complex carving of the petalled form. The radiating elements could relate to organic matter or may represent the rays of the sun. The design is also reminiscent of a plan of the great Derbyshire fallen stone circle at Arbor Low.

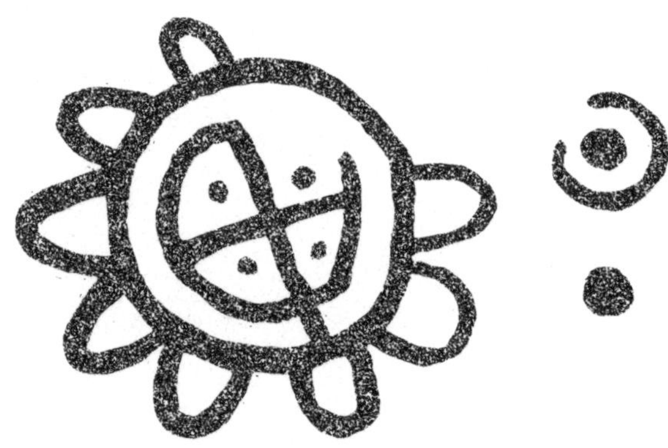

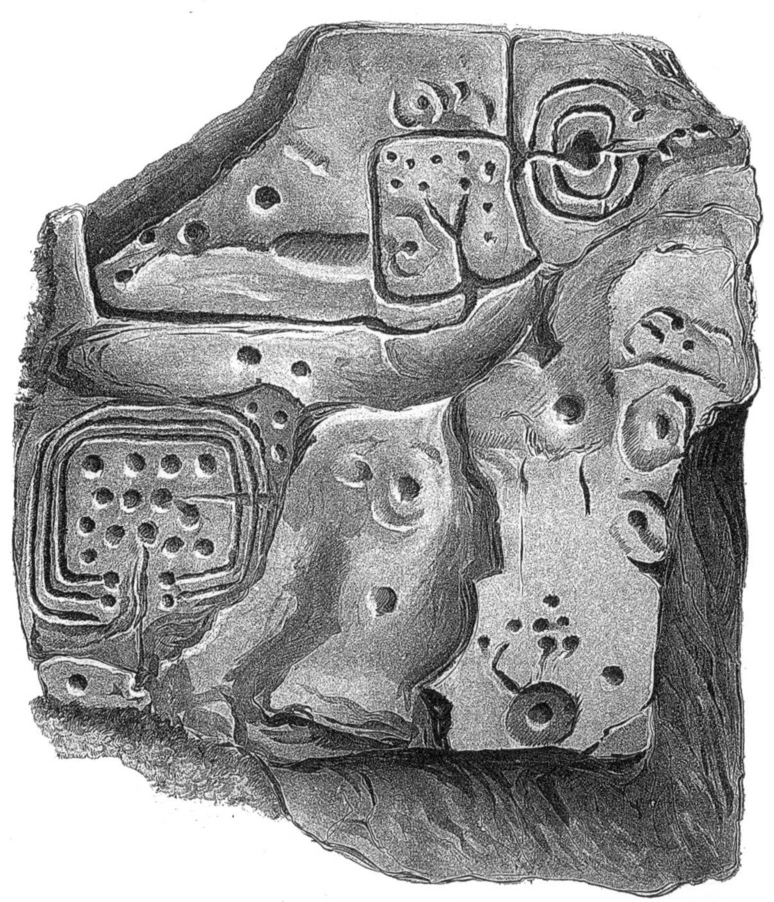

Dod Law

THE CALDERSTONES

Allerton, Liverpool

The Calderstones are the remains of a neolithic passage grave which was destroyed in 1845. They were placed on display close to the entrance to Liverpool's Calderstones Park at the time, and were then moved again in 1964 and set in a circle.

A range of elements found in rock art appear here, including carved footprints which are more common in Scandinavia and Brittany and rare in the United Kingdom.

The main motifs are cups, concentric rings, concentric rings with central cups and spirals. The spirals are both clockwise and anti-clockwise; there is some suggestion, from examples at Newgrange, that this could record some seasonal change.

It is not unreasonable to suspect that something is being recorded here and that the different combinations of symbols may have specific meanings. Likewise, the various number of cups at different sites may record different quantities.

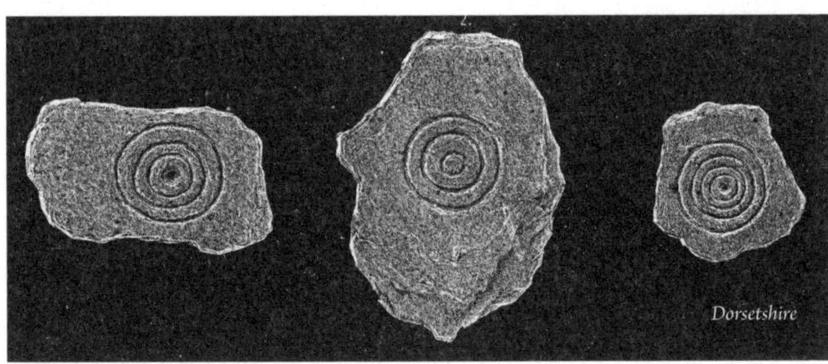

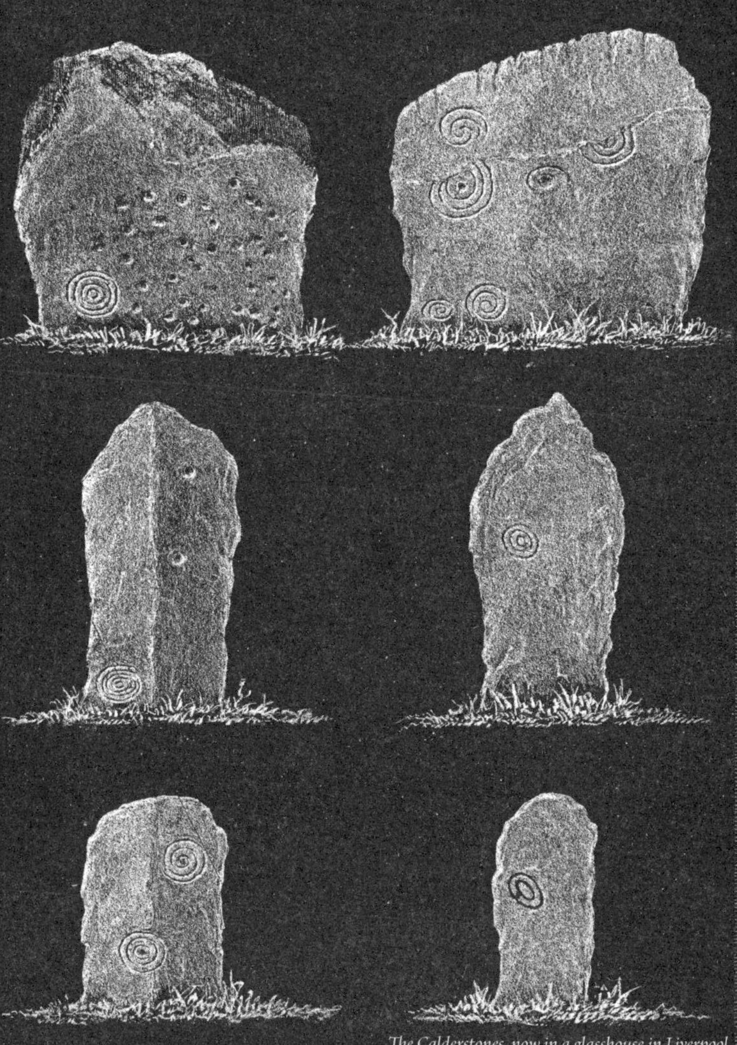

The Calderstones, now in a glasshouse in Liverpool

BALLYGOWAN CARVINGS

nr Slockavullin, Kilmartin Valley, Argyllshire

Ballygowan is one of a number of sites in the Kilmartin Valley which display considerable and complex arrangements of rock carvings. As at West Horton in Northumberland (*below*) the carvings mainly consist of cups, rings, tails and pathways but also, similarly, there are occasional anomalies such as the small horseshoe labyrinth in the bottom left of the picture (*opposite*). Some of these small elements appear so rarely that they can be considered as being specific to the site, making it even more difficult to propose a consistent explanation for these carvings.

Most of the sites in the Kilmartin area are easily accessed and well worth a visit.

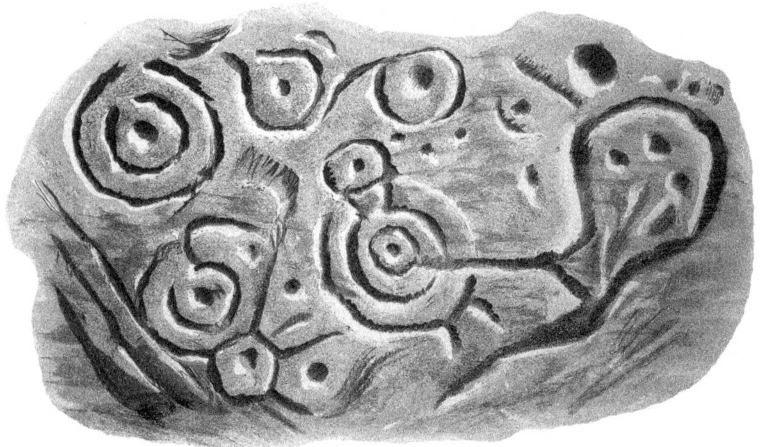

West Horton, Northumberland

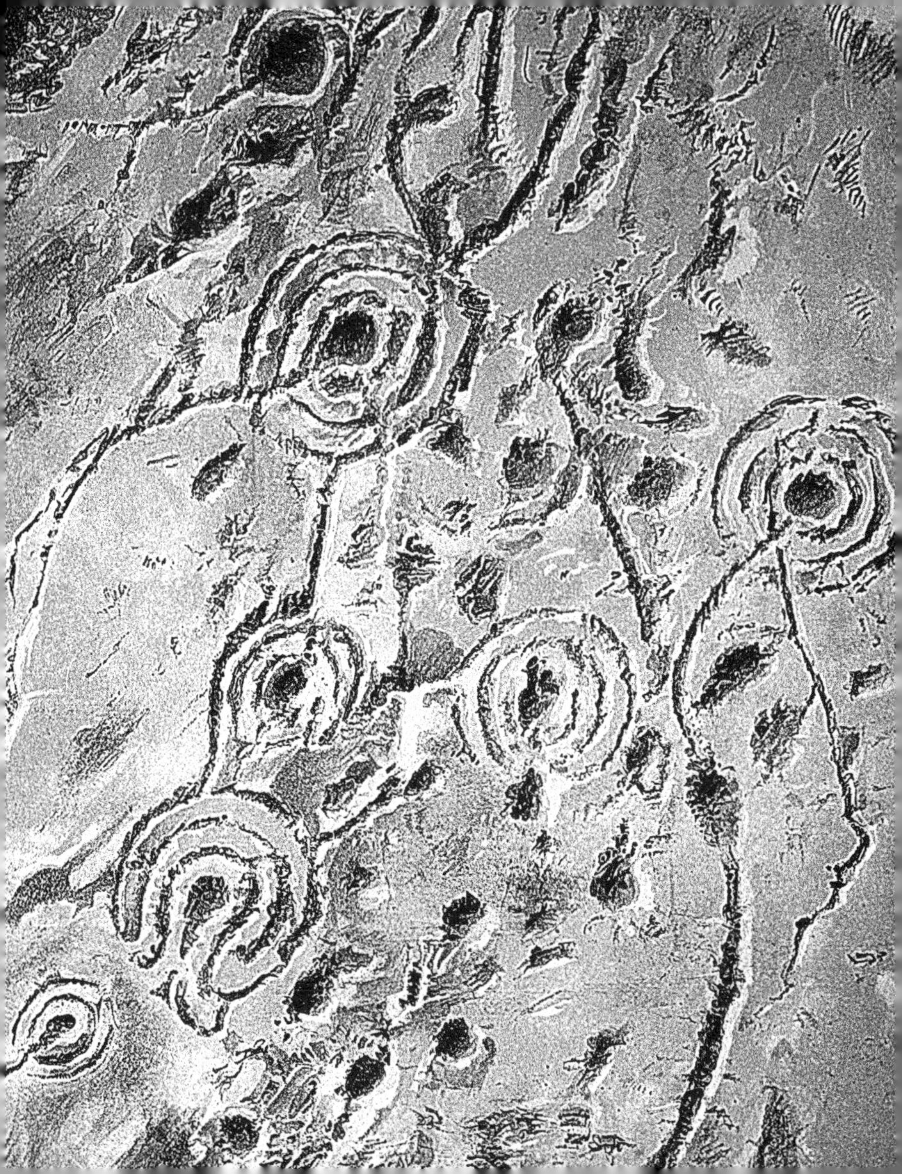

TAILS

Achnabreck and Cairnbaan, Argyllshire

So far we have seen cups and rings mainly existing either alone or in combination. It is time to introduce another interesting element, the "tail". These examples from the Kilmartin Valley show tails which extend from central cups or from the inner ring. They may join cups, pair as two tails, or join other tails, but in all of these examples the tail cuts through the rings. At other sites (e.g., Millstone Burn in Northumberland) the rings are even truncated to allow the tail to pass through.

In the example from Cairnbaan (*opposite top*), the tails vary in the way in which they interact with the cups and rings, possibly revealing some function in the style of the tail itself.

Some tails are straight and others are curved. One set of rings opposite has two tails which extend and join to enclose a single cup. These are unlikely to be arbitrary decisions and seem to indicate some specific intention.

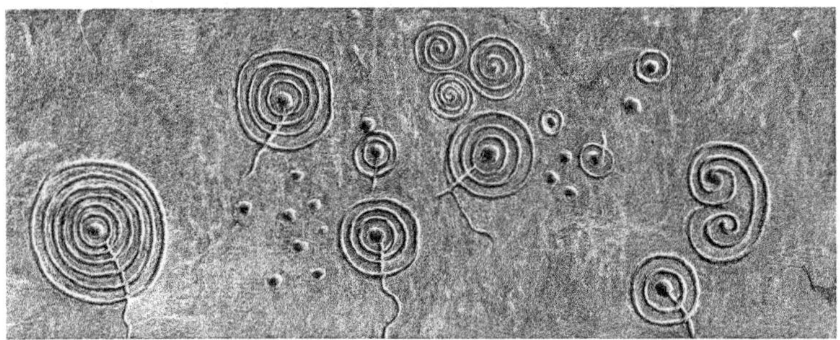

Achnabreck, Argylleshire

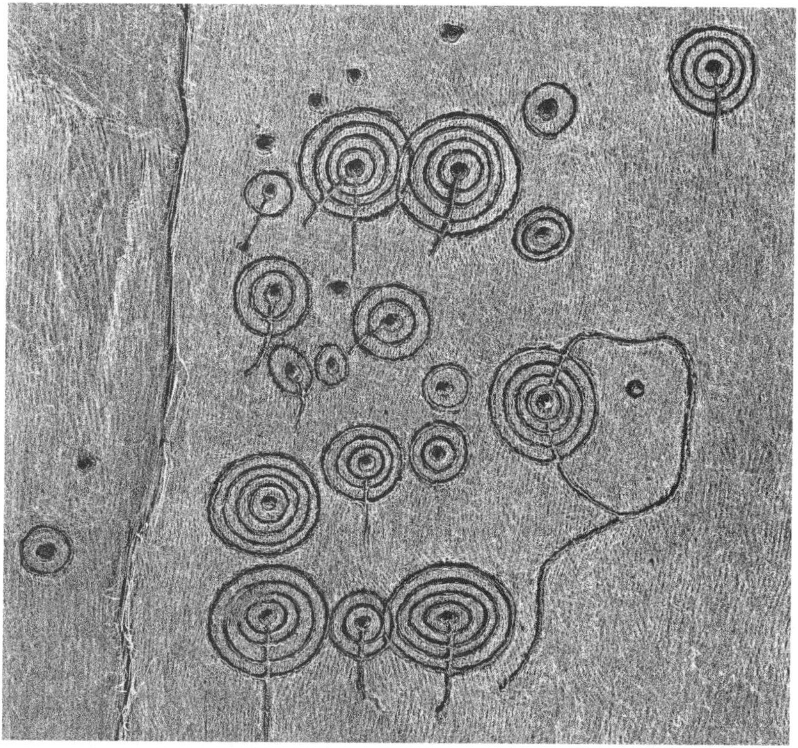

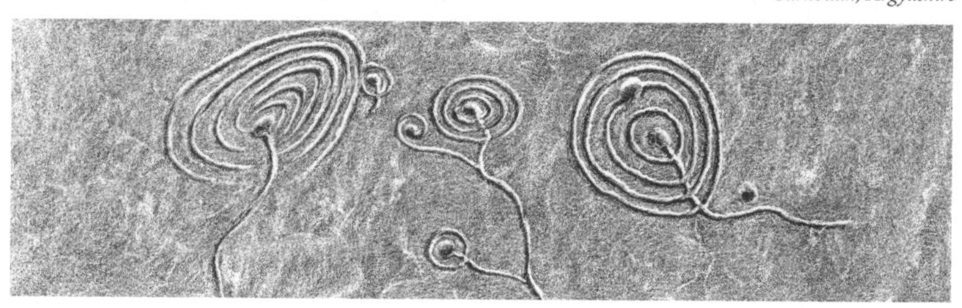

Carnbaan, Argyllshire

Achnabreck, Argyleshire

Tailed Cups With Rings

a range of examples

The tailed cup is a very prominent design element in many areas. Shown here are examples from a further range of sites. The tail gives the simple cup mark some kind of development, a movement from inside to outside, a bridge, perhaps between one dimension and another. The rings opposite are not broken, in contrast to other examples (*below left*) which allow the tail to pass through. The multiple rings help to intensify the central cup and create a more powerful design.

Evidence from Irish passage grave sites suggests that pictograms were linked with astronomical phenomena. Are these records of years perhaps, or moons? Shown on this page are tailed cups with 1, 2, 3, 4, 5, 6, 7 and 8 rings.

In the examples from Achnabreck and Millstone Burn one may notice that the tails all have the same general direction. Could this be some kind of indication of movement?

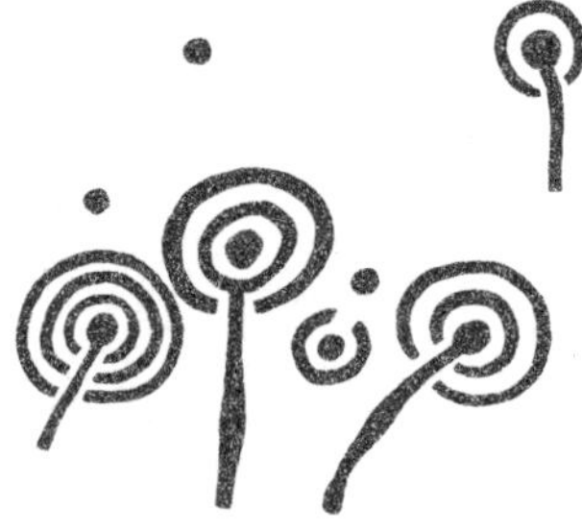

Millstone Burn, Northumberland

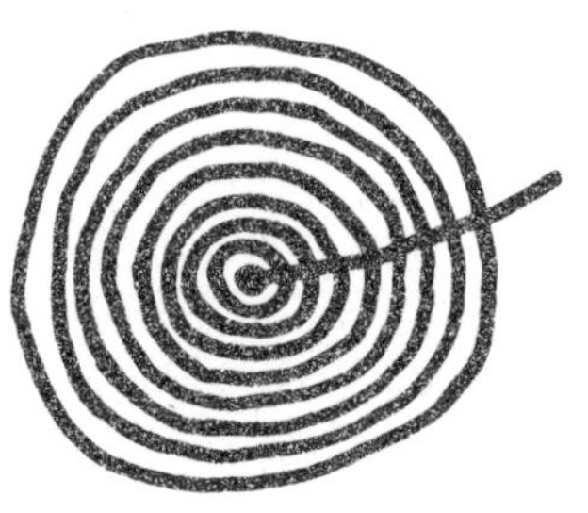

Balcraig, Galloway

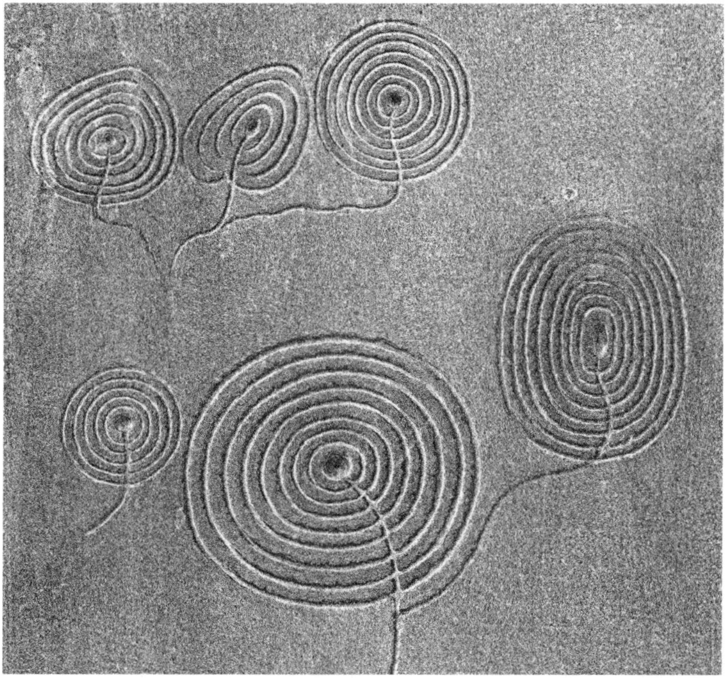

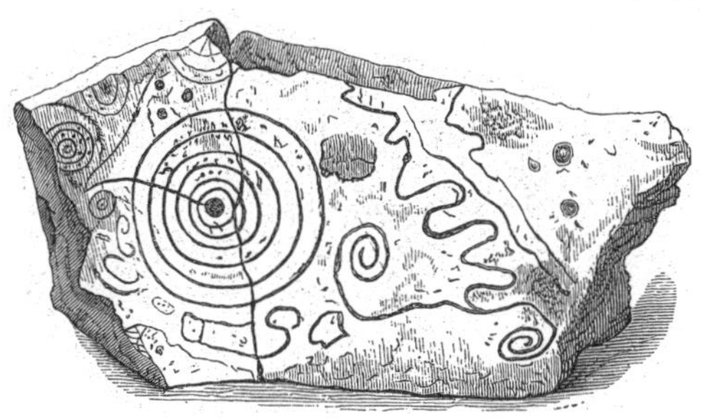

Achnabreck, Argylleshire

Coverstone of a cist, Coilsfield, Ayrshire,

CUPS, RINGS AND LADDERS
Panorama and Barmishaw stones, Ilkley, W. Yorks.

The Panorama Stone was named after the area where it was found on the edge of Rombald's Moor. The first recorded recognition of the carvings on this site was in 1850. Shortly after its discovery in 1871 by a Mr. Call and a Mr. Wagstaff, the stone was sold to a local doctor for preservation. It now stands inside railings opposite St. Margaret's Church in Ilkley.

One of the best examples of the "ladder" motif, unique to this area (*see too the Barmishaw Stone below*), it is interesting to follow the structure of the design and see how the ladders, rings and cups form the overall construction. The ladder obviously adds another ingredient to our pot. More food for thought.

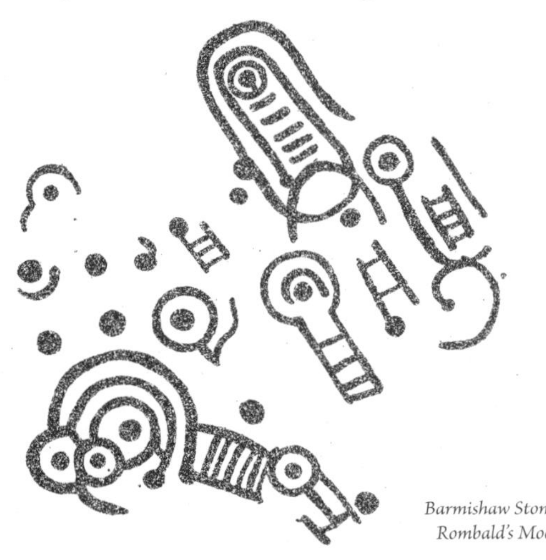

*Barmishaw Stone,
Rombald's Moor*

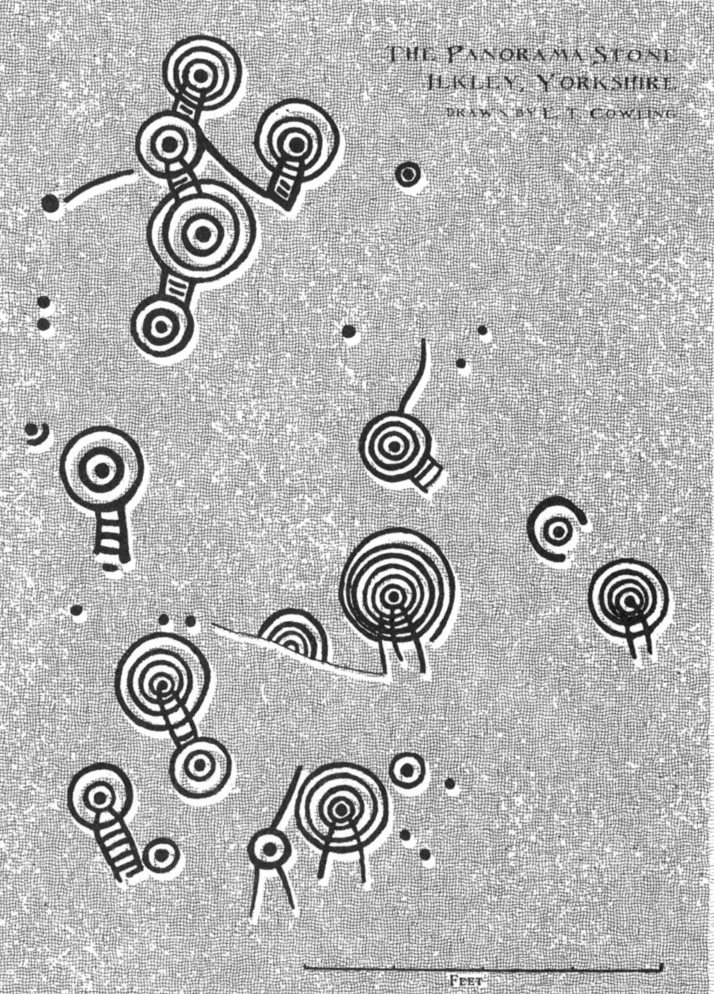

THE PANORAMA STONE
ILKLEY, YORKSHIRE
DRAWN BY E. T. COWLING
FEET

ROSETTE WHEELS WITH CUPS
Ormaig, Argyllshire.

The complex and diverse arrangement of carvings on the facing page was revealed after a great deal of time spent carefully brushing away a thick layer of pine needles.

There are two main outcrops at this location, which is probably best known for the "rosette" design (*below*). A good mixture of styles is present and some unusual "beak" motifs are attached to cups and rings. Some of the carvings are quite deep, up to one and a half inches, and the larger rings measure about a foot in diameter. This site now lies in a small clearing, deep in the forest, and is not easy to find without some direction as many of the forest roads have been relocated.

The rosette design is interesting in the fact that seven and eleven cups are enclosed and separated in this specific style. This poses the question of the significance of these numbers and what informed these decisions.

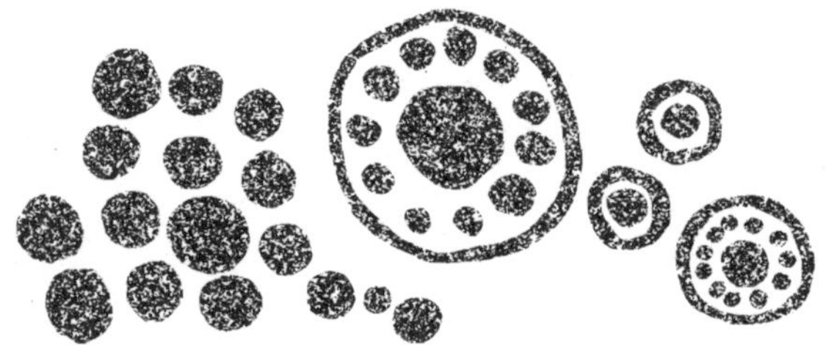

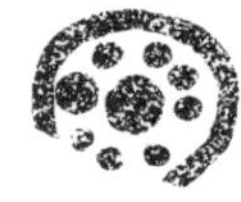

Ormaig, Argyllshire

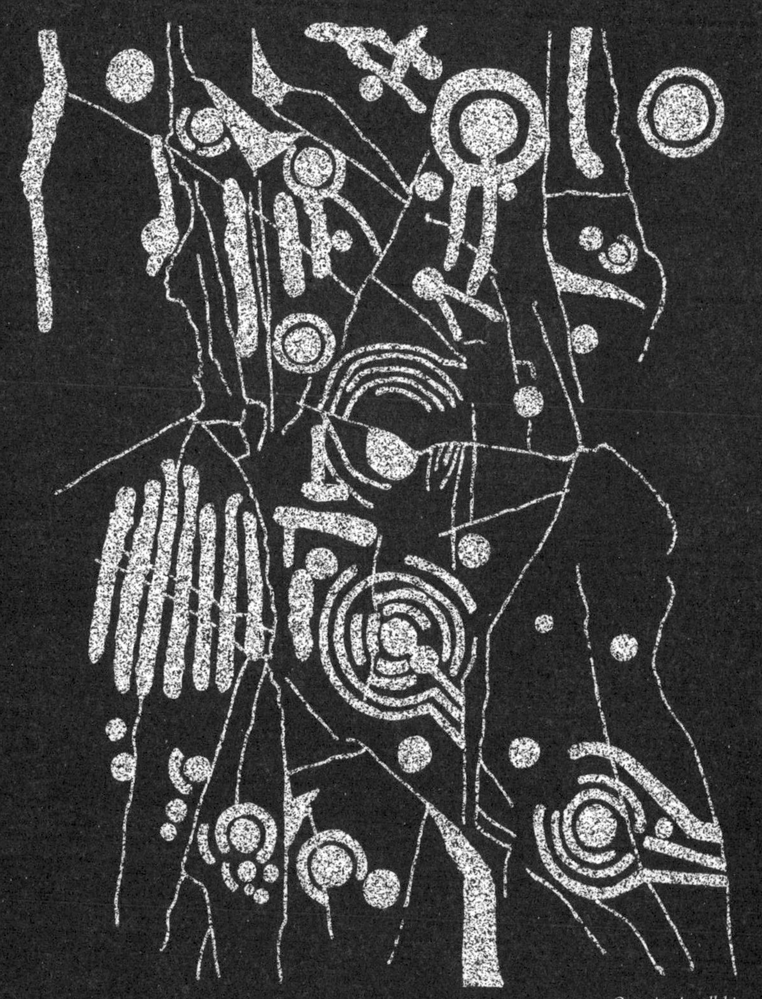

Ormaig, Argyllshire

DECORATED STONES

Long Meg, Cumbria & Barningham Moor, Co. Durham

Long Meg is one of the largest stone circles in the British Isles and Meg, the single outlier (*shown opposite*), marks the midwinter sunset position. The carvings are faint and best observed in glancing light, or at night with the use of a lantern.

The design shown below is a fascinating arrangement of cups, rings and adjoining pathways, and evokes all kinds of explanations. Perhaps there is evidence here of some ritual which has been long forgotten. The carvings are weathered and heather obscures many of the stones scattered over the moor.

The nature of the location must always be a consideration in studying and comparing styles and variations in different areas of rock art, and here the location and weathering of the examples seems to enhance the overall quality of this bleak environment.

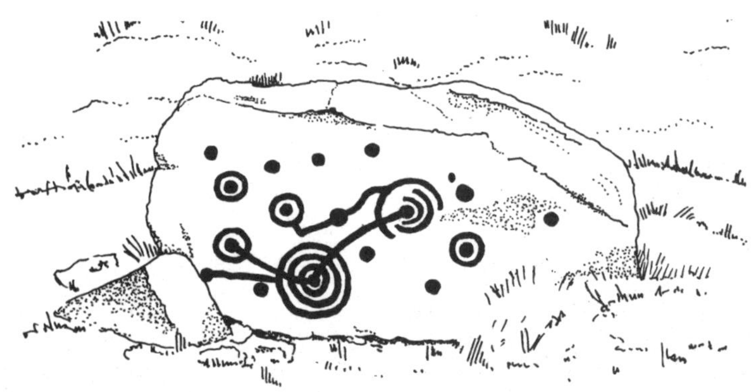

Barningham Moor, Co. Durham

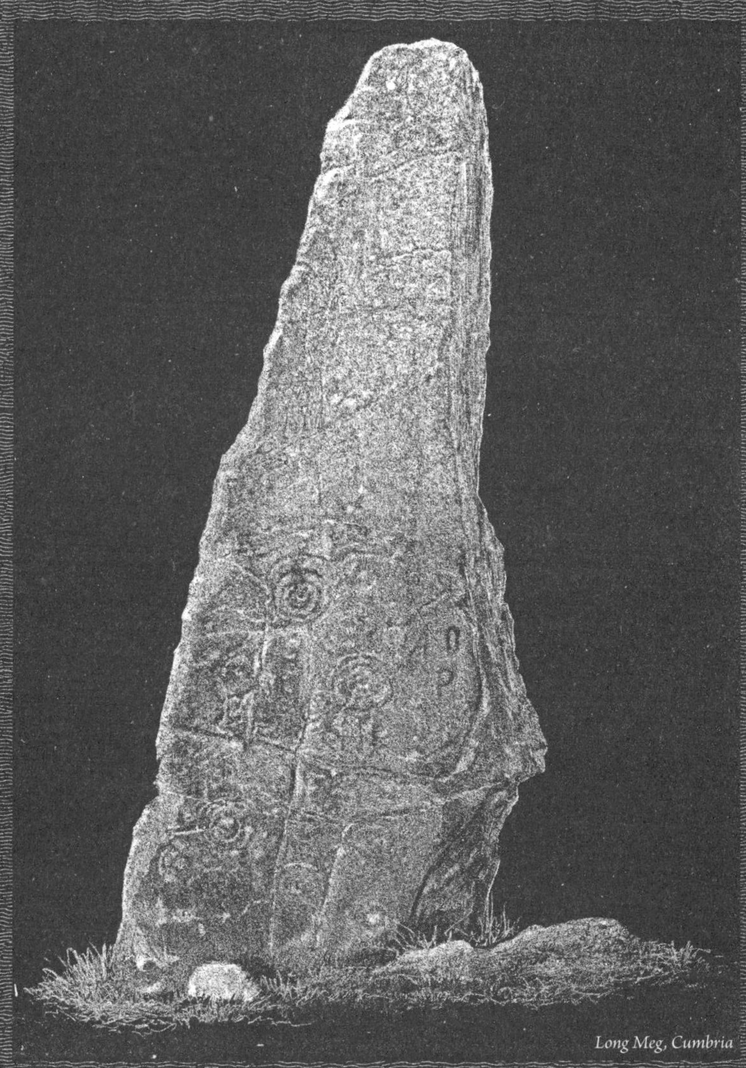

Long Meg, Cumbria

NORTHUMBRIAN DETAILS
from Dod Law, and Horton Moor

These images from the mid 19th century were originally printed using a specialist lithographic technique which employed a Balkan Limestone as a printing surface. It seems strangely appropriate that a stone process was used here to reproduce ancient marks made on stone.

The designs, from Dod Law and Horton Moor, are complex, playful and varied. A vulva-like shape (*opposite top right*), comb-like forms (*opposite lower right*) and a splayed-ringed cup (*opposite lower left*) extend the range of designs we have encountered so far.

It is hard to say quite what is going on here, and the reader may be forgiven for thinking that research has not progressed a huge amount since the time of the comment below:

"If these markings be not Celtic it is difficult to say to what age they belong"
The Rev. J Mapleton, Dunoon Castle, 1864

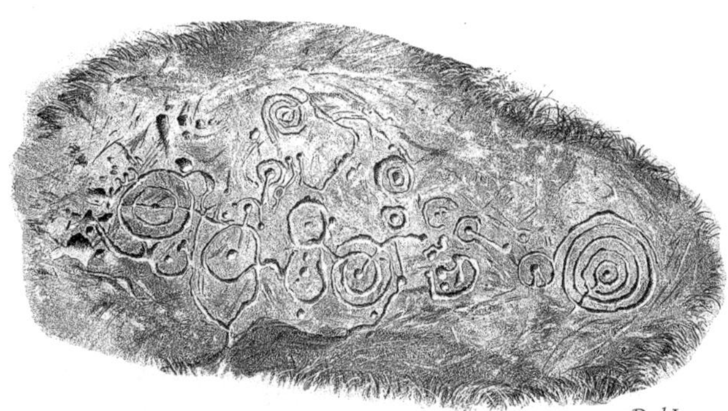

Dod Law

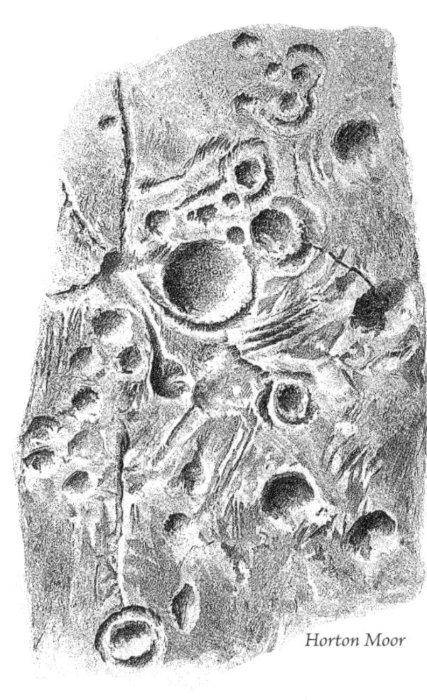

Horton Moor

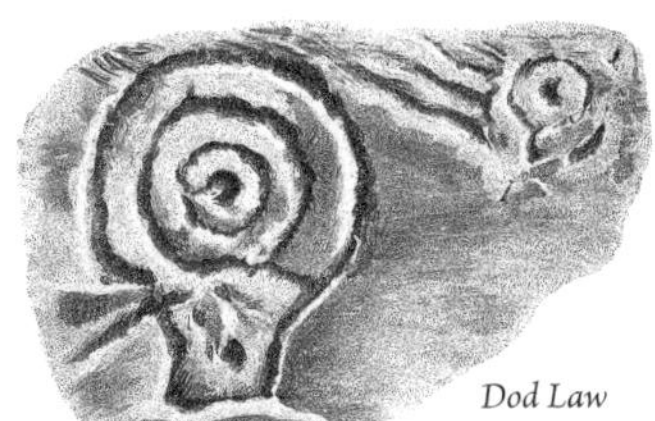

Dod Law

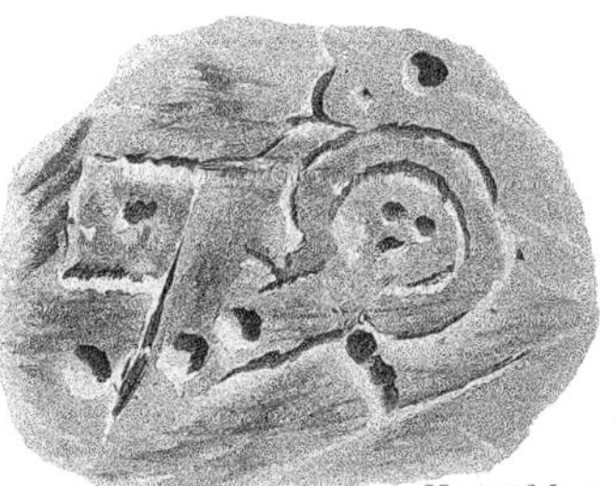

Horton Moor

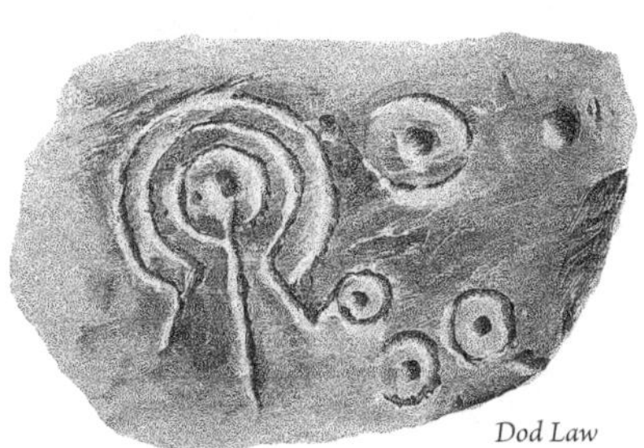

Dod Law

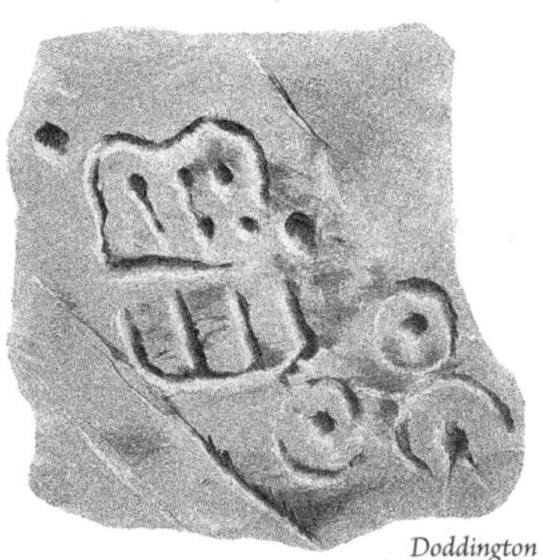

Doddington

OVERLAPPING RINGS & TAILED CUPS

Old Bewick, Northumberland

This area of the Northumberland moors lies in the shadow of the Cheviot Hills and a wealth of rock carvings are found here. The complex carvings on the famous Old Bewick stone (*opposite and below*) show how, in many examples, designs are created by "chasing" lines together. Once again there seems to be a specific purpose or meaning to these markings and the multiple rings, five in this case, intensify the overall design. One of the cups has a forked tail, a significant development from the single line, creating another route to or from the centre.

As can be imagined the possible design permutations with so many integral elements must be almost infinite.

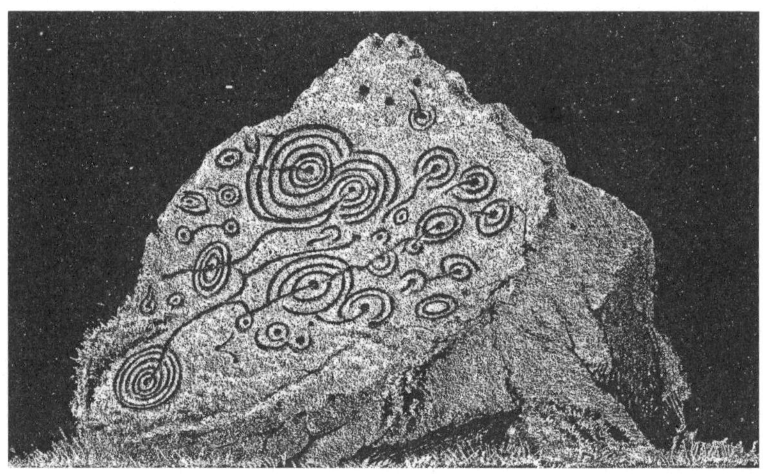

Old Bewick, Northumberland

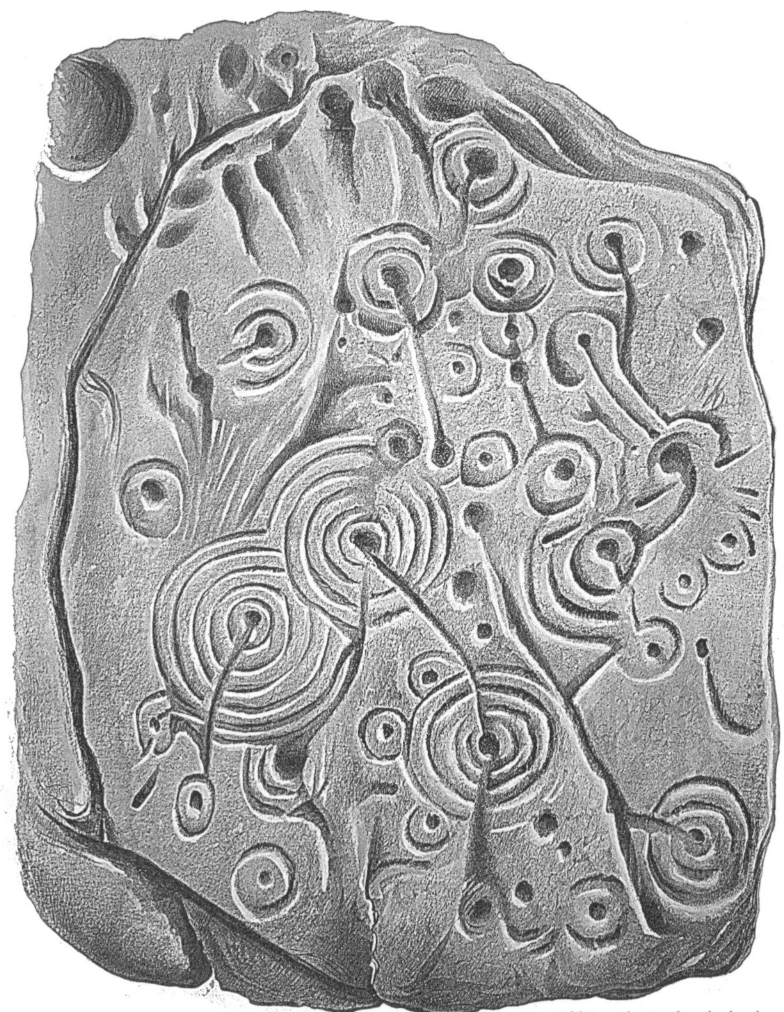

Old Bewick, Northumberland

Areas & Edges

fitting the art to the canvas

In some cases it is hard to dismiss the idea that the shape and natural structure of a rock must have influenced and controlled the overall creation of these designs. In the opposite lower right example there is something fascinating about the use of the edge of the stone, and one wonders if this may record some attempt to communicate with natural spirit elements.

Flaws in the surface of a rock are often employed and capitalised upon by petroglyph artists, but, in his 1967 article *Geometry of Cup-and-Ring Marks*, Professor Alexander Thom also suggested that considerable preparation may have been undertaken in smoothing the surface before carving.

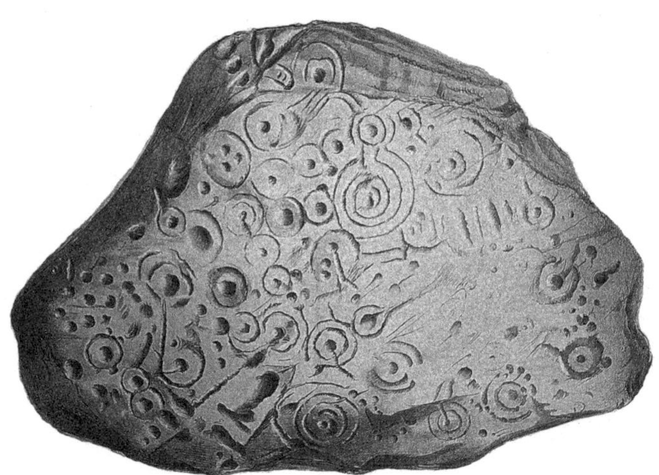

Doddington, Northumberland

38

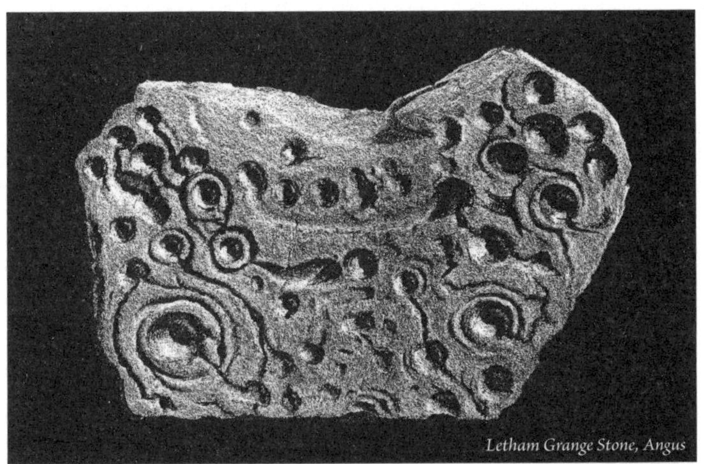

Letham Grange Stone, Angus
3
4

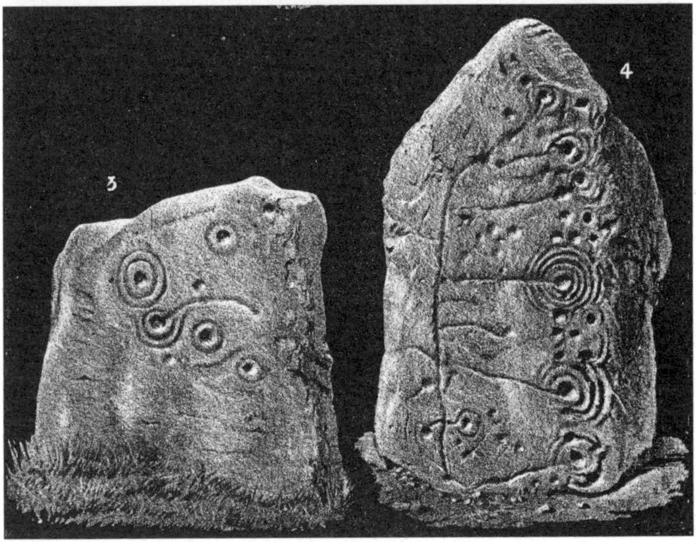

STYLES

An interesting aspect of this subject is the distinct stylistic differences which exist not only between different sites, but actually within the same area. For instance the Badger Stone on Rombald's Moor displays some variations on the cup-and-ring motif while the nearby Idol Stone has significant arrangements of simple cups following the shape of the stone with lines.

The Tree of Life, on Snowden Moor, has a even more fluid and organic approach with less emphasis on multiple rings, while Northumberland's West Horton Goddess almost looks like a human or spirit family, with the rings (some quite angular) channelled to allow the tail to pass through. It may be that these differences are due to different artists, but there is also the possibility of styles emerging over a period of time.

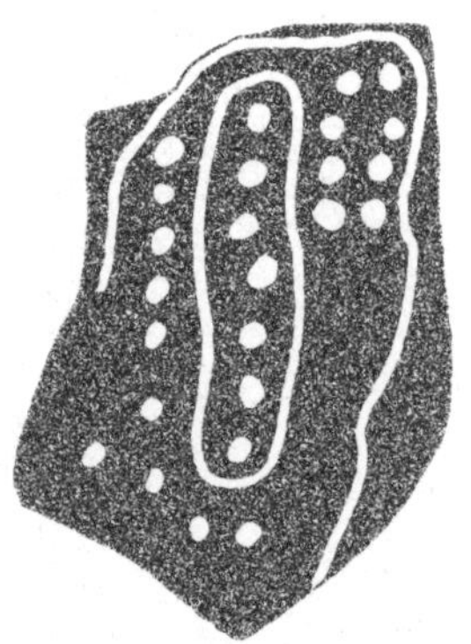

The Idol Stone, Rombald's Moor

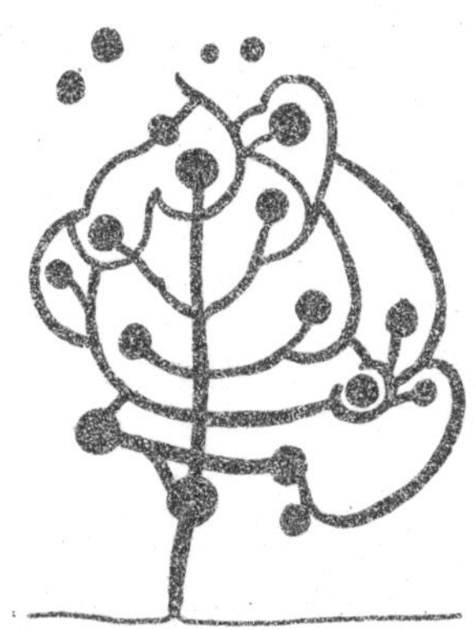

The Tree of Life, Rombald's Moor

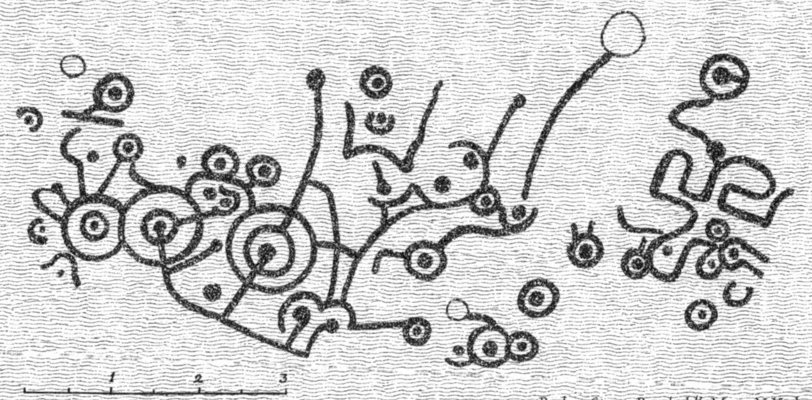

Badger Stone, Rombald's Moor, N Yorks.

West Horton Goddess Stone, Northumberland

SPIRALS

from various sites

The spiral appears regularly in megalithic art at a range of locations, often in combination with other graphic elements.

Regarded in many traditions as symbolic of the divine feminine, the spiral represents the womb, fertility, the serpent, continual change and the passage of time and evolution. Since we know that megalithic peoples were fascinated by the sun and moon, it is likely that the spiral, as a development of the circle, may also represent the sun and the passage of time. Both the sun and moon exhibit apparent spiral movement over time, rising and setting in different places every day, and their journey was referred to as "spiralling" by ancient astronomers.

Spirals can have many arms, and the number depicted might have been important to ancient astronomer-artists, possibly representing a number of days or months. In Martin Brennan's reclassification of neolithic symbols the spiral is one of the primaries, and can be left- or right-handed as well as retrograde (reversing internally). Brennan suggests that the direction of the spiral may indicate "the beginning, growth" (left hand spiral) or "the end, decay" (right hand spiral).

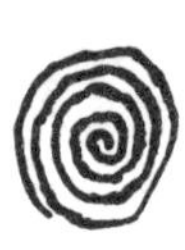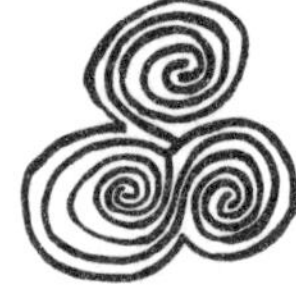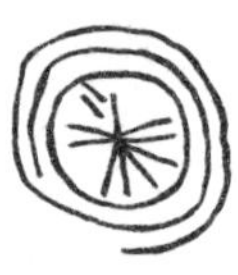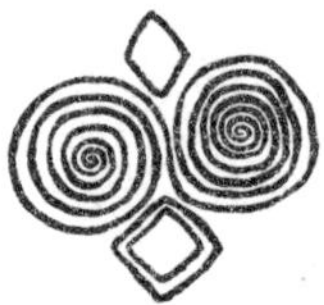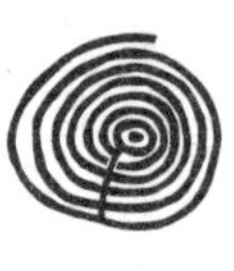

Spirals from Newgrange (1,2 & 4) and Loughcrew (3), Co. Meath, Eire, and Cauldside Burn, Kirkcudbright (5)

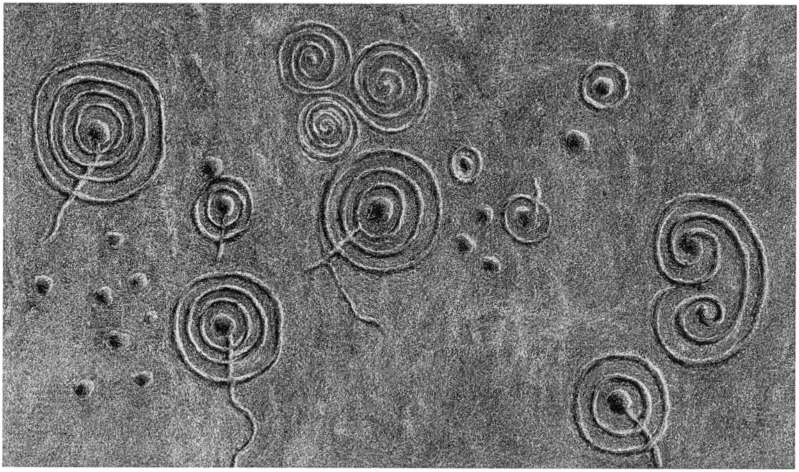

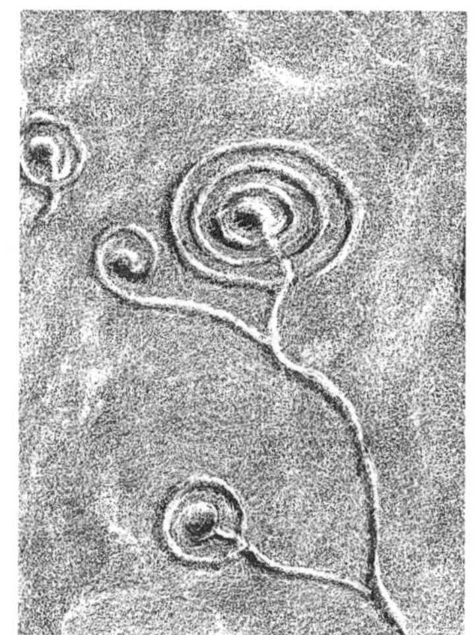

Achnabreck, Argylleshire

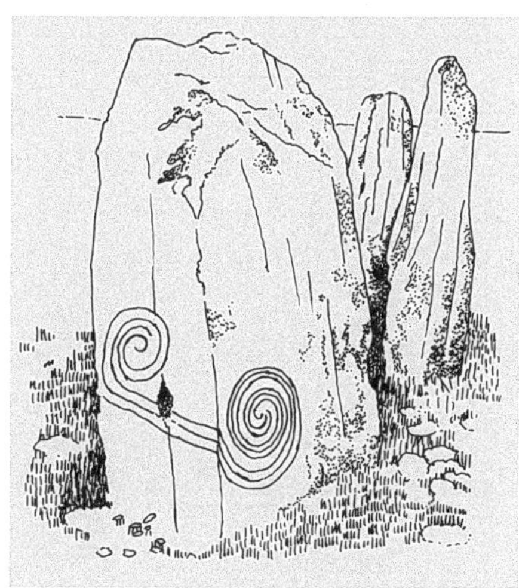

Temple Wood Stone Circle, Kilmartin Valley

Sharp Angles

triangles, diamonds and zig-zags

The triangle and its associated structures have long been dynamic elements which have been employed by many cultures and religions. In Christianity, Judaism, Tibetan Buddhism, Zen and the more recent Bauhaus, the triangle has been seen and employed as a powerful fundamental element, often associated with a range of qualities and attributed colours. Xenocrates, the Greek philosopher, suggested that the triangle was a symbol for God, and in Christianity it represented the Holy Trinity. It is associated with fire and strength but also with harmony and balance.

The zig-zag could be a reference to, or a symbol for, water but given the complexity of other nearby elements, this may be too simple an explanation of its meaning in this context.

The cist cover from Carnwarth is interesting in that it exhibits differing styles, simultaneously displaying typical ring marks beside the stylised triangular motifs.

These examples show that angular designs were not local to one area or tradition. Whether such simple and universal devices arose spontaneously or through communication between different communities is a matter for debate.

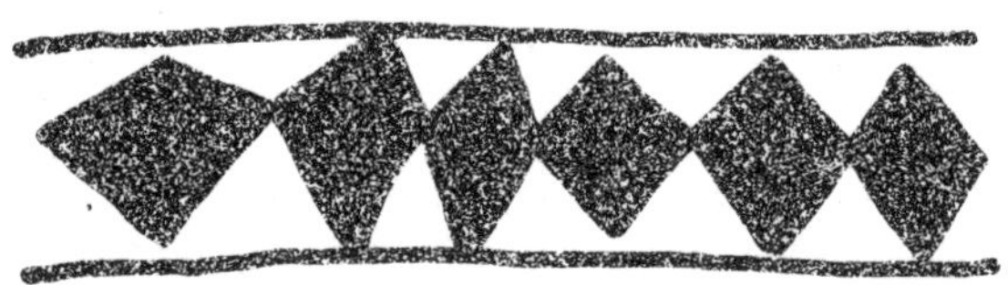

Newgrange, Co. Meath, Eire

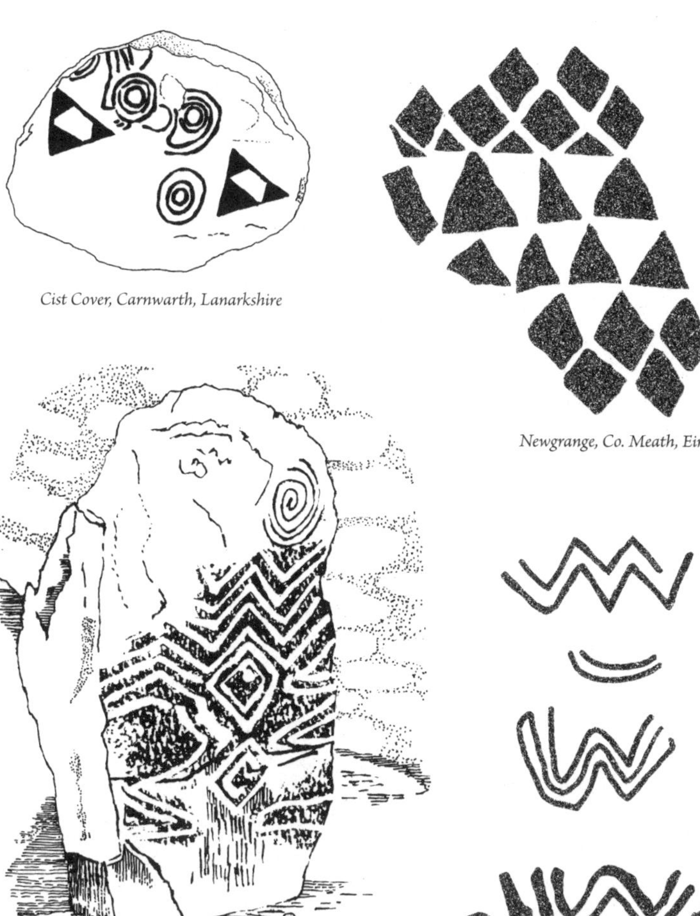

Cist Cover, Carnwarth, Lanarkshire

Newgrange, Co. Meath, Eire

Barclodiad y Gawres, Anglesey

Newgrange, Co. Meath, Eire

45

STARS AND SUNS

Loughcrew & Knowth passage grave, Co. Meath, Eire

The top two drawings on the page opposite resemble and may indeed represent stars. Below, three flower motifs from the same stone are thought to symbolise suns, solar years, or possibly solar year counts (like the 8-year Venus cycle). Or they could possibly represent the sun at different times of the day or year.

There is an increasing awareness and body of research concerning the employment of astronomical alignments by ancient cultures. Evidence is mounting that many of these early communities used the risings and settings of specific heavenly bodies in an intelligent and informed way.

Martin Brennan's drawing (*lower opposite*) is an excellent example of how some of these elements are combined: cups rings, spirals and stars. The diagonal line of cups across the centre seems to suggest a lunar count. The ability to record and apply this kind of information in such an aesthetic manner must have taken great diligence and intelligence.

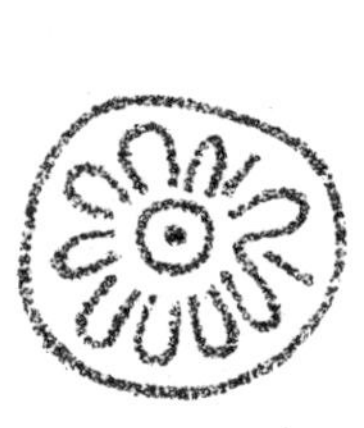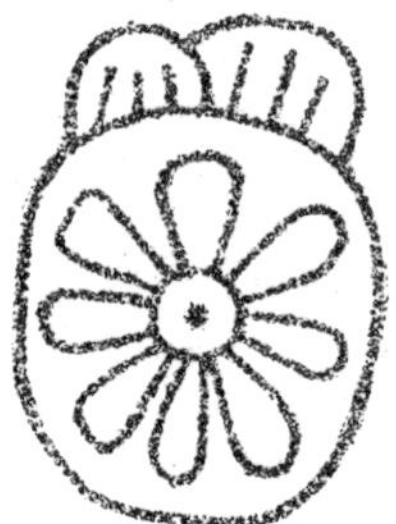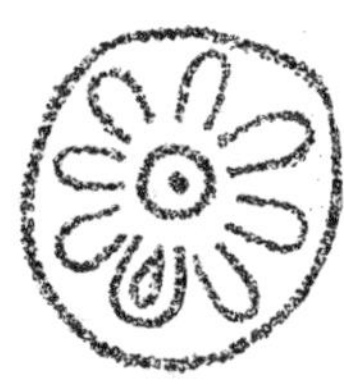

Suns from Cairn T, Loughcrew

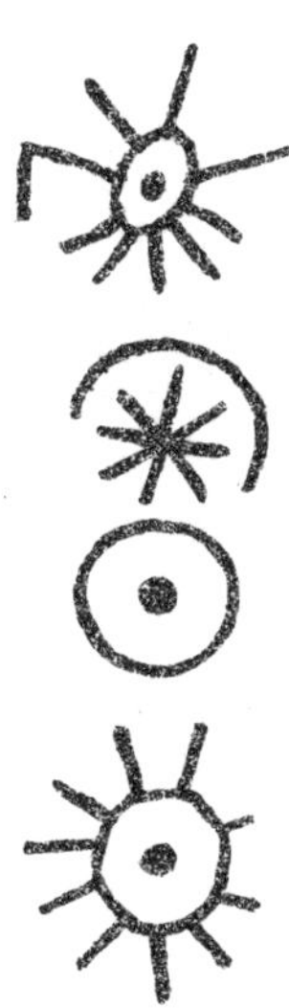
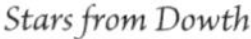

Stars from Dowth

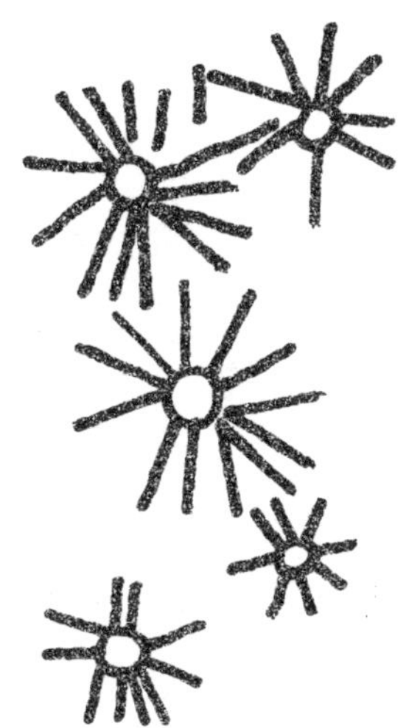

Stars from Knowth

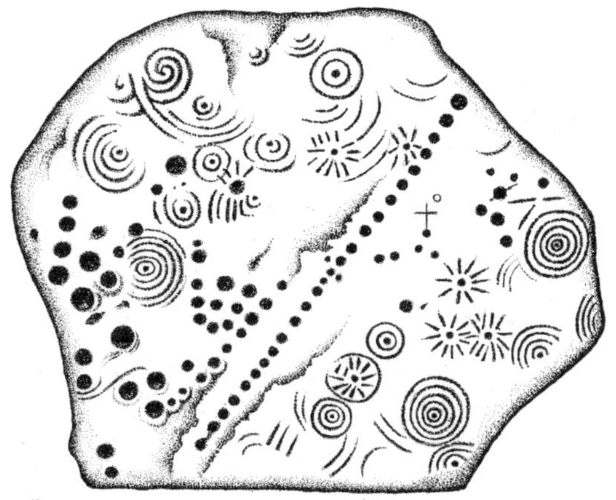

Chamber Roof Slab, near Sess Kilgreen, Co Tyrone

SYMBOLS

Loughcrew passage grave, Co Meath, Eire

The complex mixture of symbols shown here extends the study of rock carvings into an area of greater sophistication in the application and meaning of visual design. The effective minimalism of cup and ring marks, although still visible here, is now accompanied by designs which may have a much more representational root. These could be stars, flowers, leaves and water, but the random arrangements give little clue as to whether the elements are interrelated or simply the outcome of incremental addition. Some of the more representational elements resemble tribal art from Africa or Australia.

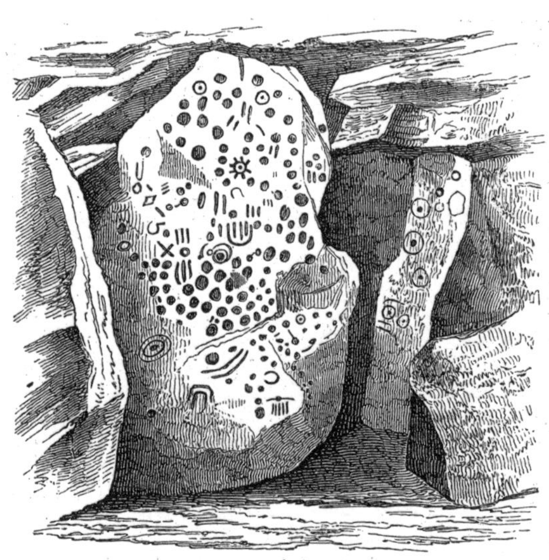

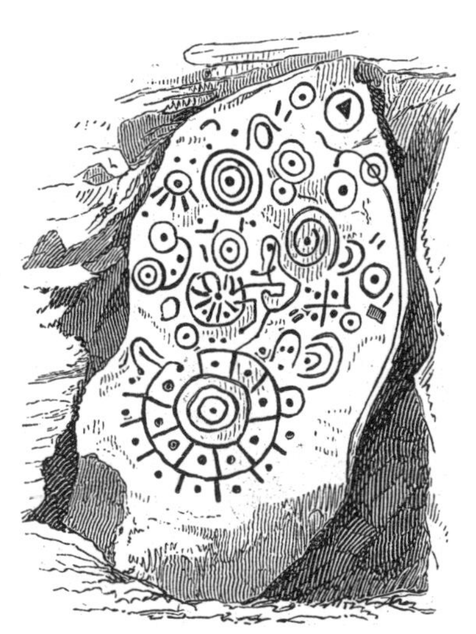

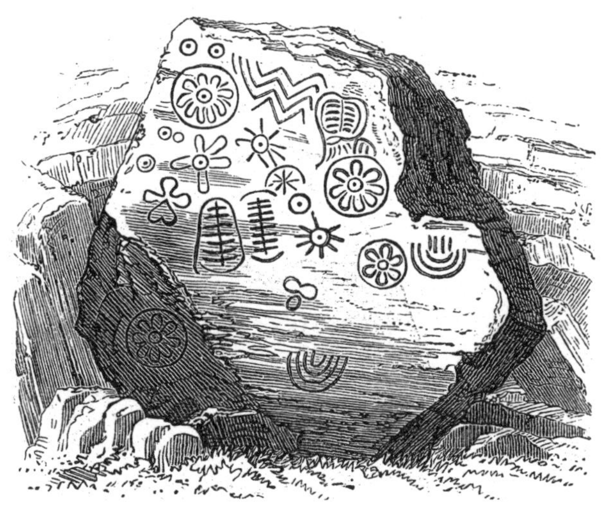

IRISH MEGALITHIC ART

the Boyne valley, Co Meath

The sheer quantity and quality of megalithic art in the Boyne Valley in Co. Meath emphasises the importance of these sites to those that built them over 5000 years ago.

After extensive research, published in his excellent 1980's book *The Stars and the Stones*, Martin Brennan, who made the drawings of the stones opposite, concluded that most of the art in this area is concerned with astronomical data and alignments. He clearly identified a range of symbols as representing the sun, the moon and the passage of time.

Of Kerbstone 15 at Knowth N L Thomas observes:

> *"the stone is a unique statement, an exact 365 day, sixteen month, four-week month, five-day week solar calendar"*

The illustration by Brennan below is of Knockmany Passage Grave, now enclosed, an example of how rock art was integral to the megalithic culture.

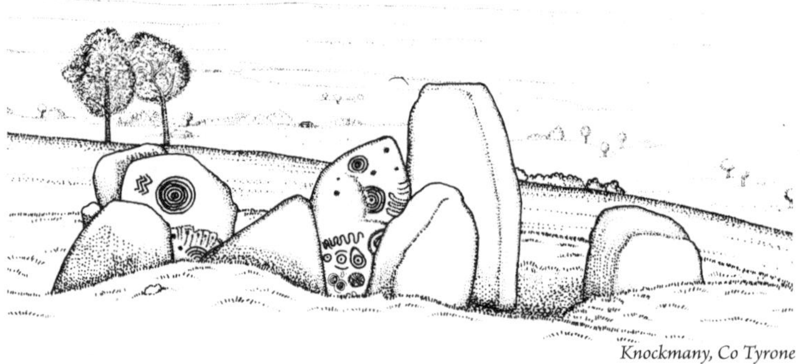

Knockmany, Co Tyrone ·

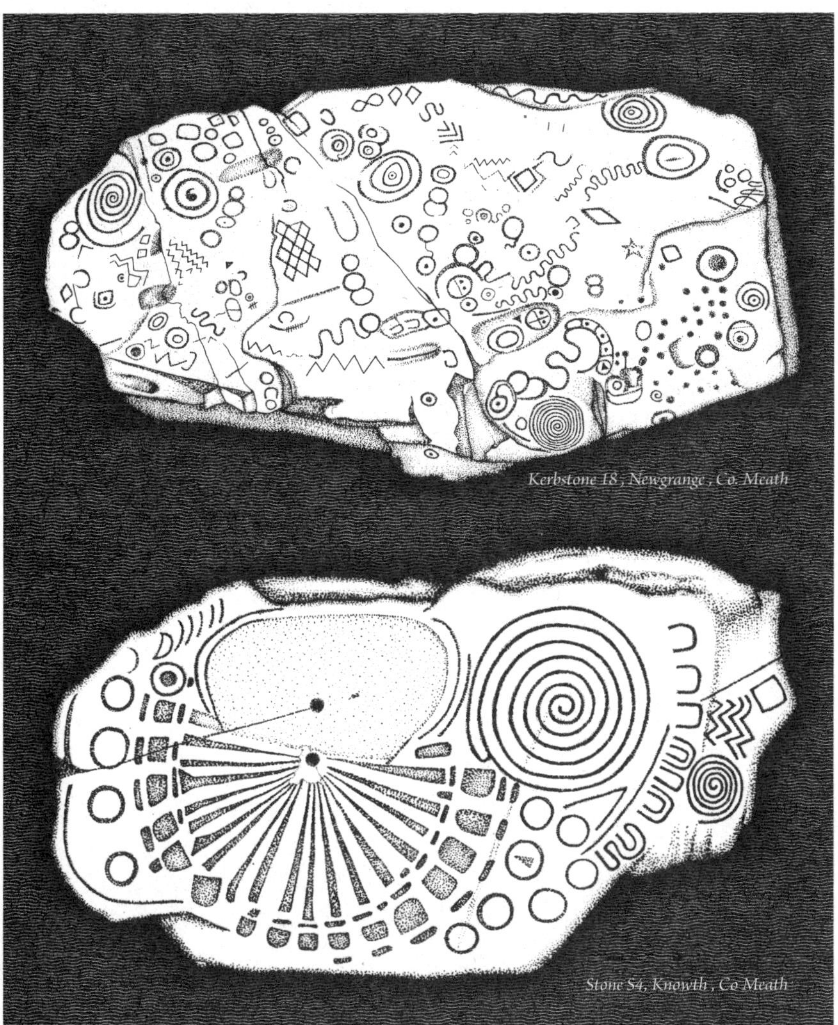

Kerbstone 18 , Newgrange , Co. Meath
Stone S4, Knowth , Co Meath

NEWGRANGE PASSAGE TOMB
Newgrange, Co. Meath, Eire

At 9 am on December 21st the dawn rays of the winter solstice sun enter the chamber at Newgrange and illuminate a specific range of pictograms, slowly moving from one to another over 15 minutes as the sun swings round. A special roof box above the entrance allows the sun to penetrate right to the back wall.

Two huge kerbstones (*one shown opposite top*) are directly aligned at the front and back of the mound, their central grooves also aligning with the winter solstice.

Built between 3300 and 2900 BC, 500 years before the Great Pyramid of Giza, Newgrange is an amazing construction, beautifully decorated and a testimony to the skills and dedication of those who built it. The conjunction and balance of opposites here, of midsummer and midwinter, Sun and Moon, light and dark, life and death, embody the whole interplay of the forces and energies of regeneration (*lower pictures by Martin Brennan*).

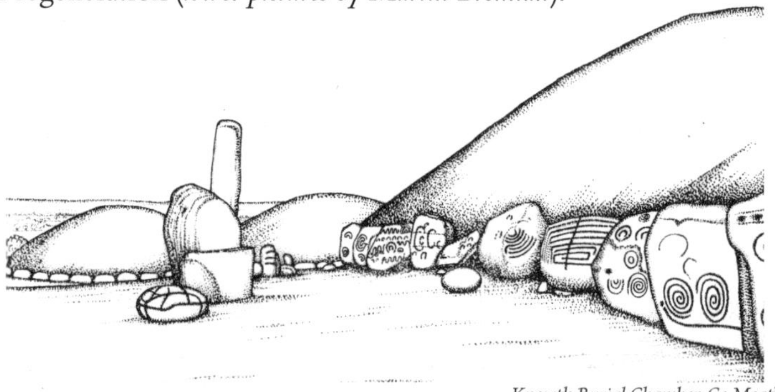

Knowth Burial Chamber, Co Meath

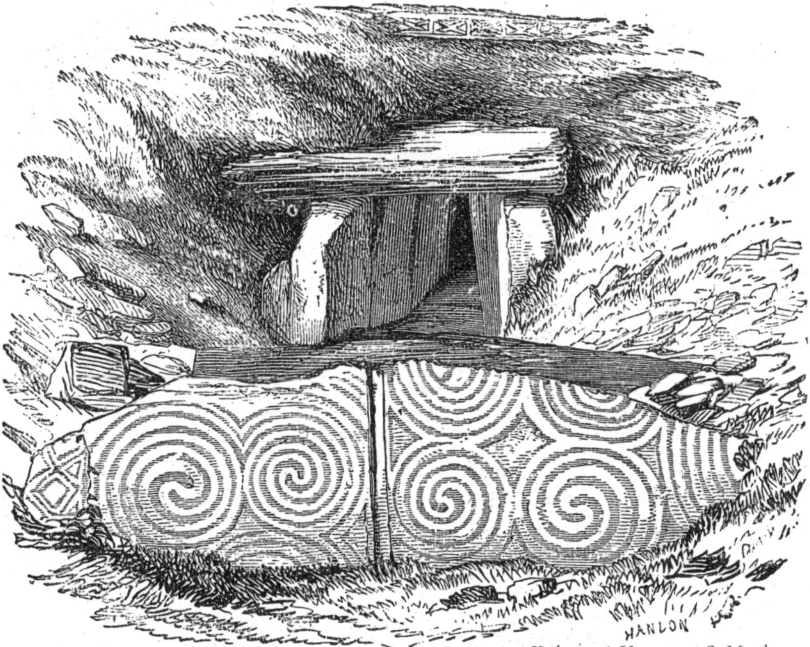

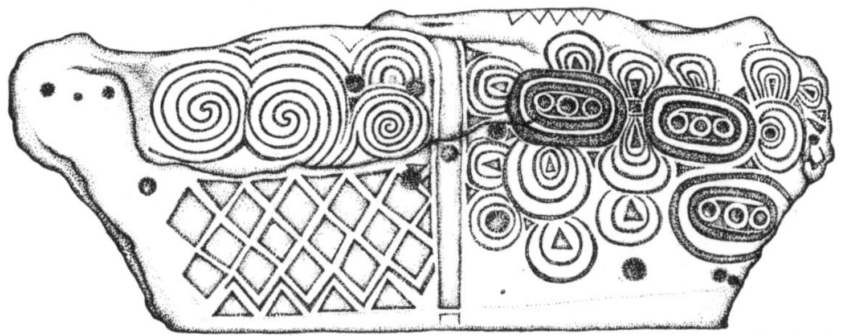

Kerbstone 1, Newgrange, Co Meath

Kerbstone 52, Newgrange, Co Meath

GAVRINIS
Gavrinis Cairn, Morbihan, Brittany

Across the Channel, the extensive 3000 BC carvings at Gavrinis are particularly interesting in the way that the flowing, abstract designs cover and take account of the shapes of the stones on which they are made. Are these simply decorative patterns or do they contain clues to some ancient forgotten perception?

It may be that the stones were decorated before being positioned but it is certain that they are intended to create a specific impact on the inside of the cairn and to perform an intended visual function. It is interesting to conjecture as to who the viewer would be as these structures are primarily houses of the dead. Did they possibly have a wider function?

In the end very little is really known about these important archaic sculpturings. Merely their age. I hope I have conveyed some of their mystery, majesty and beauty in this little book.

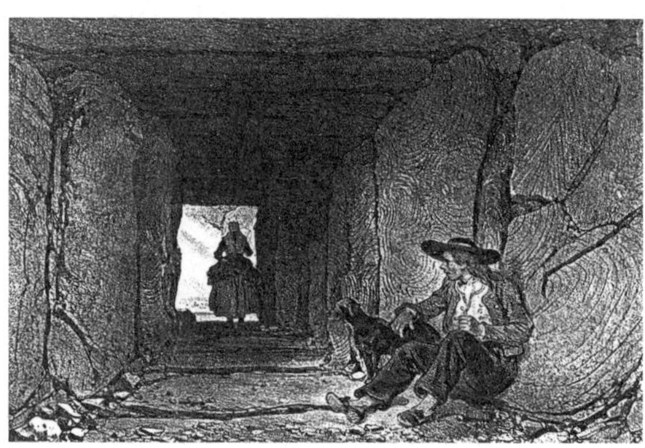

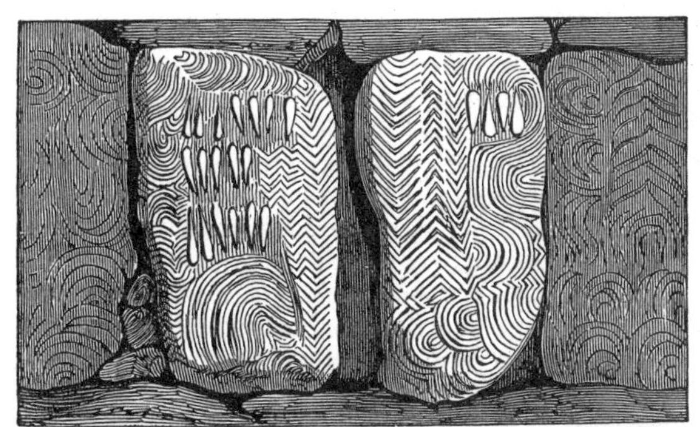

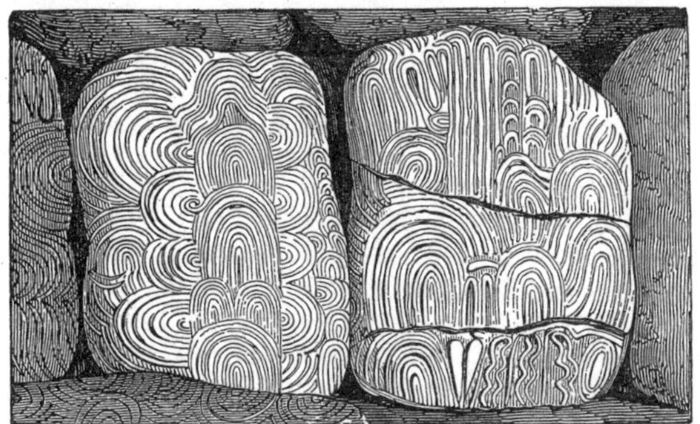

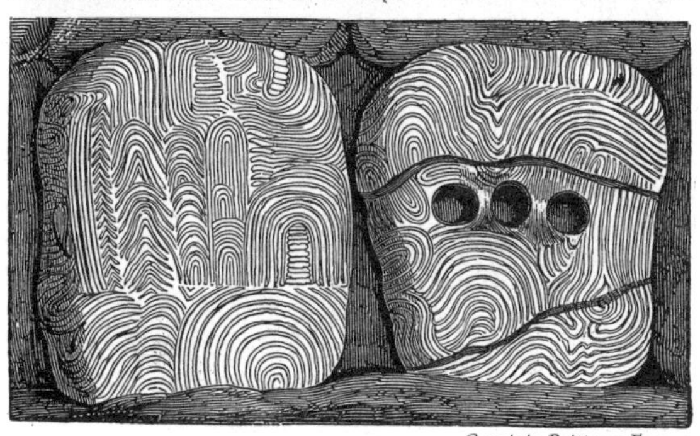

Gavrinis, Brittany, France

55

Interesting Sites & Locations

SITE	OS REF.
DERBYSHIRE	
Rowtor Rocks, Peak District	SK 235 622
COUNTY DURHAM	
Barningham Moor, Barnard Castle	NZ 054 083
NORTH YORKSHIRE	
The Idol Stone, Ilkley Moor	SE 132 459
Panorama Stone, Ilkley Moor	SE 114 472
Rombald's Moor, Ilkley	SE 145 441
Hangingstone Quarry, Ilkley Moor	SE 128 467
NORTHUMBERLAND	
Barmishaw Stone, Rombald's Moor	SE 112 464
Dod Law	NU 0041 3178
Dod Law	NU 001 324
Roughting Linn	NT 983 376
Millstone Burn	NU 1189 0521
Millstone Burn	NU 1142 0528
Old Bewick	NU 078 216
SCOTLAND	
Caulside Burn, Galloway	NX 528 573
Ballymenoch, Kilmartin Valley	NR 832 964
Balcraig, Galloway	NX 377 443
Ormaig, nr. Kilmartin	NM 822 027
Temple Wood, Kilmartin Valley	NR 827 978
Carnwath	Nat. Mus of Scot.
Clava Cairns, Inverness	NH 753 440
WALES	
Barclodiad y Gawres, Anglesey	SH 329 707
IRELAND	
Loughcrew, Co Meath	N 567 770
Newgrange, Co Meath	O 015 721
Knowth, Co Meath	N 997 734
Dowth, Co Meath	O 023 736

*If you have access to the internet and want more rock carving information,
Julian Cope's site www.themodernantiquarian.com is excellent, as is Andy Burnham's
www.megalithic.co.uk and Stan Beckensall's archive at http://rockart.ncl.ac.uk*

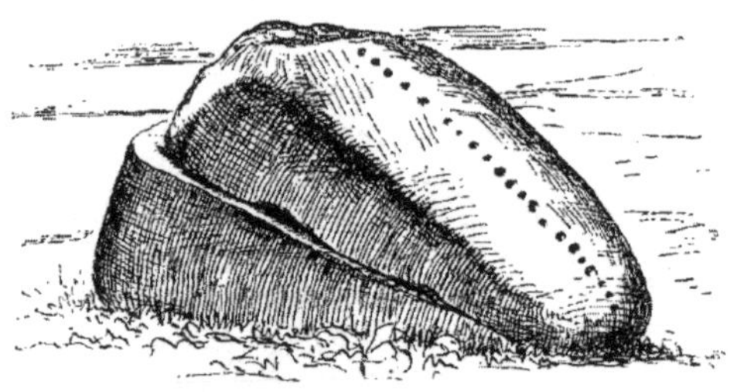

The Witch's Stone, on Tormain Hill, Ratho.